FOSTERING THE USE OF EDUCATIONAL TECHNOLOGY

Elements of a
National Strategy

Thomas K. Glennan • Arthur Melmed

Critical Technologies Institute

Prepared for the
Office of Science and Technology Policy
and the U.S. Department of Education

RAND

Since early 1992, at the direction of the president and vice president, federal officials have been exploring ways to encourage greater and more effective use of modern technology in the nation's schools. As part of this effort, RAND's Critical Technologies Institute (CTI), in support of the Office of Science and Technology Policy, conducted analyses of existing federal research and development activities related to technology for education and training and participated in the planning activities of the Committee on Education and Training of the National Science and Technology Council.

In 1994, the Goals 2000: Educate America Act directed the Secretary of the U.S. Department of Education to develop a national long-range technology plan for actions promoting higher student achievement through the use of technology in education. The CTI was asked by the Office of Science and Technology Policy and the Office of Technology of the U.S. Department of Education to under-take a number of activities to support the development of this plan.

The CTI held four workshops dealing with important policy areas to be considered in the national plan. These have been documented in four papers:

- *Technology and Teacher Professional Development,* James Harvey and Susanna Purnell (eds.), DRU-1045-CTI, RAND, Santa Monica, CA, March 1995.

- *Planning and Financing Educational Technology,* James Harvey (ed.), DRU-1042-CTI, RAND, Santa Monica, CA, March 1995.

- *The Market for Educational Software,* James Harvey (ed.), DRU-1041-CTI, RAND, Santa Monica, CA, May 1995.

- *The Costs and Effectiveness of Educational Technology: Proceedings of a Workshop,* Arthur Melmed (ed.), DRU-1205-CTI, RAND, Santa Monica, CA, November 1995.

In addition, the CTI analyzed the technology-related costs of a set of schools making extensive use of technology. The results of these analyses appear in

- *The Cost of School-Based Educational Technology Programs,* Brent Keltner and Randy Ross, MR-634-CTI/DoED, RAND, Santa Monica, CA, 1996.

This report draws on the discussions in these workshops, the analysis of costs, and reviews of existing literature to identify key elements of national strategy and federal policy that will contribute to effective use of technology by the nation's schools. It should be of interest to federal policymakers concerned with education and technology policy as well as educators and others concerned with the use of technology in elementary and secondary education.

CTI was created by an act of Congress in 1991. It is a federally funded research and development center (FFRDC) within RAND. CTI's mission is to

- provide analytical support to the Executive Office of the President of the United States
- help decisionmakers understand the likely consequences of their decisions and choose among alternative policies
- improve understanding in both the public and private sectors of the ways in which technological efforts can better serve national objectives.

Inquiries regarding the CTI may be directed to

> Bruce W. Don
> Director
> Critical Technologies Institute
> RAND
> 2100 M Street, N.W.
> Washington, D.C. 20037-1270

CONTENTS

FIGURES

TABLES

In 1983 there was about one computer for each 125 students in the nation's public schools. By 1995, there was a computer for each nine students. In 1994, the nation's schools spent about $3 billion on computer- and network-based technology. Additional funds were spent for other kinds of equipment such as video players, facsimile machines, and telephone lines as well as for technology-related training. Nationally, new federal legislation has emphasized the importance of educational technology and leaders have called for actions to ensure the access of all schools to the national information infrastructure. Many states and local school systems have appropriated or reallocated funds, or issued bonds to finance acquisition and installation of technology in schools. As has been the case in other parts of American society, major changes associated with the growth of information technology are clearly under way in our schools.

At the same time, much of America is in the midst of significant efforts to reform and improve the performance of its education system. The president and the governors, in a historic agreement, established broad national education goals in 1989. National political, business, and community leaders have called for higher standards and educational practices that enable virtually all students to meet these standards. Because of the significant growth in the importance of being competitive in the international economy, educational outcomes relating to the capacity to effectively work, continue to learn, and be effective citizens are receiving greater attention. States and communities, to varying degrees, are pursuing these goals.

Technology can play a key role in this reform. Numerous examples exist where computer- and network-based technology has been used to

- tailor learning experiences more sharply to learner needs and abilities.

- provide students with access to resources and expertise outside the school, both enriching their learning and extending the time devoted to learning

- support more authentic assessment of a student's progress

- assist schools in managing and guiding the learning activities of their students.

Moreover, as Louis Gerstner, CEO of IBM, has said, "[information technology] is the force that revolutionizes business, streamlines government and enables instant communications and the exchange of information among people and institutions around the world." If technology becomes widely infused in a school, it seems probable that it can play analogous roles in education. Technology can be the "revolutionary force" that instigates and supports reform by teachers and administrators at the school level.

The authors of this report believe the continuing growth in the presence of technology in schools presents an important opportunity to a nation seeking improved performance from its schools. The report seeks to identify principles that should guide the actions of public officials, educators, and others concerned with using technology to improve the performance of schools and school systems. Prepared as a result of participation by RAND's Critical Technologies Institute (CTI) in federal efforts to plan a research agenda and develop a national educational technology plan, it is based upon a series of workshops, interviews, and literature reviews. The report considers three major questions:

1. What do we know about the use and effectiveness of computer- and network-based technology in elementary and secondary education?

2. What major strategies should the nation consider as it seeks to make effective use of technology in its schools?

3. What are the most important roles for the federal government to play?

While we present a variety of important findings and recommendations, perhaps the most important is that the nation seek to build its strategies on lessons from its early experiences. The significant levels of investment made in recent years mean that some schools have already acquired and put substantial amounts of technology into effective use. A key role for federal, state, and local officials is to tap the experiences of these "pioneer" schools for lessons that can increase the probability that continued investments in educational technology will be well used.

CURRENT USE AND EFFECTIVENESS OF EDUCATIONAL TECHNOLOGY

The growth in use of technology by schools is strong; schools are adding equipment and developing connections to the national information infrastructure at a high rate. The expanded penetration of computers in schools, noted in the opening sentences, is projected to continue. Despite this rapid growth, surveys suggest that the average school still makes limited use of computers and substantial numbers of schools have very limited access to technology of any kind. Instances of deep, schoolwide use, espoused by advocates of technology-supported instruction, are comparatively rare. Rather, use of technology to significantly affect classroom practice tends to be limited to small groups of teachers who are excited by the potential that they feel technology has to motivate their students or to access new resources. As has been the case with past attempts to introduce technologies such as radio, film, and television into schools, computers and telecommunications remain marginal contributors in most settings.

A small number of "pioneer" schools with ubiquitous technology show the potential for restructuring provided by educational technology. In these schools, students, teachers, and administrators report taking new roles. Technology has been used to manage complex, standards-related instructional processes in ways that have previously been achieved by only the most skilled teachers. It facilitates communications among teachers so they can collaborate more effectively. In some of these schools, technology is also used to support communications among schools, students, and parents, fostering an improved partnership among these actors, and greater accountability and public support.

Effectiveness

Research and practice suggest that, appropriately implemented, computer- and network-based technology can contribute significantly to improved educational outcomes. Most of this experience is in small trials in one or a few settings, but research has aggregated these experiences into a significant body of literature that illuminates the potential of technology in a variety of settings.

Research on "reinventing" whole schools through ubiquitous use of technology is not common. In part, this reflects the rarity of such schools—schools that may provide computers for each child and extensive networking that encourages collaboration and communication. The research that exists is promising but not conclusive. The schools represented at our CTI workshops were producing results valued by their community, but they clearly were exceptional schools. It remains to be seen whether similar results can be sustained as increasing numbers of schools acquire similar levels of technology.

Equity

According to surveys carried out several years ago, the availability of technology in schools serving poor, minority, and special-needs populations does not appear to lag substantially behind the averages of schools taken as a whole. Past federal, state, and local funding and policies appear to have mitigated extreme differences in the average availability of computers among special populations. In particular, federal compensatory education programs have supported the acquisition of substantial technology for schools serving disadvantaged populations, particularly at the elementary school level.

In contrast, the disparities in home possession and use of computers are substantial among families with differing incomes, parental education, and ethnicity. To the degree that technology comes to be used to extend the amount of time spent in learning activities outside the schools, these disparities will have considerable consequences for the achievements of students from different family backgrounds. If the disparities persist, access to technology is likely to become one more element in the array factors that cause a student's educational attainment to be highly correlated with the socioeconomic status of his or her family.

Costs

The costs of ubiquitous use of technology are modest in the context of overall budgets for public elementary education, but actually moving to such use would require significant and potentially painful restructuring of school budgets. We investigated the costs of a small number of schools making extensive use of technology. The estimated annual costs related to technology use in those schools ranged from about $180 to $450 per student. In 1994–95 the current expenditure per student in average daily attendance was $5,623. If $300 were viewed as a target level of funding per student for technology-related costs, about 5.3 percent of the current budgets of schools would need to be allocated to technology. On its face, this seems a level that should be attainable.

However, we estimate actual expenditures per student in 1994–95 to be $70, or one-quarter of the $300 figure. The bulk of school budgets is devoted to personnel costs; in most districts funding for materials and supplies is very restricted and provides little opportunity for further reallocation to technology. To support levels of expenditure equal to $300 per pupil will require reallocations of funds that have proven very difficult to achieve in public schools and/or increments in funding that taxpayers in most jurisdictions have been reluctant to provide.

Such reallocation will be possible only if the public and the educational community come to feel that technology is essential to meeting their objectives for student learning. Information about and demonstration of the importance of technology are critical to continued growth in technology's use. In our view, developing and disseminating such information constitutes a core role for the federal government.

Challenges

Other challenges need to be met if effective, widespread use of technology is to be achieved. Two seem particularly important: equipping teachers to effectively exploit technology for the benefit of their students and assuring a plentiful supply of high-quality content software.

Both the observations of experts at our workshops and the results from past research strongly suggest that teachers must acquire new skills needed to operate in technology-rich environments. Current professional development policies do not encourage teachers to acquire such skills. Similarly, few programs preparing people to enter the teaching profession were viewed as dealing effectively with technology. If the nation fails to aggressively address this problem, the significant investments in technology itself are likely to have marginal impacts on the overall conduct of schooling.

Educational software provides a somewhat different challenge since it is developed and sold in commercial markets. Widely available software tools such as text processors, spreadsheets, and network browsers play key roles in schools with ubiquitous technology, but they are largely developed in response to broader commercial markets. This is not the case for content software, which provides important and structured sources of information and/or opportunities for practice. Such software, keyed to the content standards of states and local districts, is important for realizing the full potential of computers.

The market for educational materials, as traditionally structured, offers limited incentives for entrepreneurial development of content software. The market is fragmented and governed by a variety of materials adoption practices. Even if a high proportion of schools acquires a product, the volume of sales is small. This is particularly true with the more specialized subject areas characteristic of much of secondary education.

However, this situation may be changing. New alliances among publishers and a spectrum of software developers, the rapid growth in the national information infrastructure coupled with its potential for changing the manner in which software is distributed, and the emergence of new entrepreneurs all promise significant changes in the manner in which schools acquire and use instructional materials and content software.

ELEMENTS OF A NATIONAL STRATEGY TO EXPAND THE USE OF TECHNOLOGY IN EDUCATION

Why should the nation develop elements of a national strategy concerning educational technology? After all, large investments are being made in such technology, and equipment, software, and practice are evolving rapidly. In our view, the reason for seeking a strategy lies in the nation's past experiences with attempts to capitalize on technology or to promote one or another reform in education. All too frequently, these efforts foundered because implementation was flawed, communities and teachers were not adequately involved, or inadequate resources were devoted to the task. Some attention to these lessons will help the nation increase the probability that investments in technology will yield improved outcomes in terms of student learning.

A full strategy, engaging all relevant interests, is surely too ambitious. However, we propose several strategic principles to guide the nation as it moves to introduce additional information technology into its schools. As additional experience is accumulated, more explicit principles can be developed. The proposed principles are simple and straightforward—intended to shape an ongoing activity rather than spur new activities.

1. *The introduction of educational technology into schools should occur as a component of a broader effort of school reform to improve the learning of all children.* Such reforms include developing and implementing high standards for all students, creating assessment systems that effectively measure the attainment of such standards, restructuring the roles of teachers, and adopting instructional practices that increase students' motivation and time to learn. In the absence of a persistent and intensive effort to maintain a focus on improving student learning, the promise of technology will be lost. In the absence of changes in the incentives governing the behavior of schools and teachers, it is unlikely that student learning will improve. Technology without reform is

likely to have little value; widespread reform without technology is probably impossible.

2. *Over time, the costs of educational technology should be built into school budgets as a normal component of recurring costs.* Major responsibility for financing and implementing technology clearly lies with state and local school authorities. These authorities are likely to incorporate technology as a recurring cost only as technology demonstrates its value in schools and districts that are early adopters.

3. *Public authorities at all levels should work with the private sector to see that all schools have access to the national information infrastructure at reasonable costs.*

4. *All levels of government should monitor the access to technology that exists for traditionally disadvantaged populations and be prepared to do what is possible to ensure equality of access.* If, as we expect, learning expands beyond the walls of the school and the length of the school day, the inequalities in access to computers and telecommunications outside the school will become an important additional barrier to achieving the traditional national goal of providing equality of educational opportunity to all children.

5. *All levels of government should seek to learn and use the lessons from schools and school districts that pioneer in the creation of technology-rich learning environments.* The early adopters of technology can help smooth the way for those who follow.

6. *The federal government's role should involve leadership, dissemination of information on effective practice, fostering the development of organizations capable of assisting schools to make effective use of technology, and funding of research and development.*

THE FEDERAL ROLE IN FOSTERING EFFECTIVE USE OF EDUCATIONAL TECHNOLOGY

While the major burdens for acquiring and using educational technology lie with schools, school systems, and states, there are important and traditional roles the federal government should play. These encompass four major classes of activities.

1. Continuing advocacy and leadership for school reform, emphasizing the potential that technology has for improving student performance.

2. Creating and disseminating high-quality information concerning the effective deployment and use of education technology.

3. Fostering the development of assistance organizations that will help schools and school systems successfully implement effective, technology-enabled schools.

4. Sustaining a vigorous and relevant program of research and development related to educational technology.

Leadership and Advocacy

Even in these times of political turbulence and change, most Americans look to leaders of the federal government for guidance. Thus the federal government can bring together state and local leaders, executives of private firms, community leaders, or representatives of key interests to discuss common issues or to map collaborative efforts.

Leadership can also be provided by identifying and recognizing outstanding performance. One of the most powerful national programs affecting the private sector has been the Baldridge Awards for quality management. These awards have inspired many companies to undertake extensive efforts to improve the quality of performance of their entire organization. Various programs to recognize effective schools have had similar, if less well publicized, effects. There is every reason to believe that effectively publicized programs that appropriately recognize technology-enabled schools, effective educational software, or specific classes of educational technology applications can provide strong guidance and incentives to schools, school systems, and the private sector.

Creating and Disseminating Better Information for Reformers Concerning Technology

A traditional federal government function has been to survey activities across districts and states to understand what is working and what pitfalls and barriers exist. In the area of educational technology, the Department of Education might gather data and assess and disseminate information on

- effective strategies for financing educational technology at the state and district levels

- exemplary program and schoolwide implementations of technology as a means of restructuring schooling

- effective applications of technology to the training and professional development of teachers

- the progress in connecting schools and classrooms to the national information infrastructure

- the access of various special populations of students to technology.

Some of these are tasks for the National Center for Education Statistics; others should be carried out by the Office of Education Research and Improvement (OERI). Many examples of effective practice would presumably be found in the pioneer schools and districts that are emerging. Special attention should be devoted to them. The Department of Education should coordinate these efforts, perhaps through the Office of Educational Technology or the Planning and Evaluation Service.

Fostering the Development of More Effective Assistance Organizations

It is important to distinguish between the dissemination of information discussed in the previous subsection and the provision of assistance to schools, teachers, and school systems. RAND's experience in evaluating school reform programs persuades us that there is an important function of organized assistance for the transformation of schools generally and for the development of schools with technology-enabled learning environments in particular. This assistance should be concrete, timely, and sustained. It should be provided on terms that the recipients find helpful, rather than on terms convenient to the provider.

The Department of Education should identify the qualities of effective assistance and inventory the potential sources of assistance related to technology. Working in conjunction with other department offices, particularly OERI, it should guide the department's support of assistance organizations so as to further the effective school use of educational technology.

The medium is part of the message. The Department of Education should actively seek opportunities to model and exploit the use of technology as a tool for providing assistance.

Support for Research, Development, and Demonstration (RD&D)

RD&D support is traditionally one of the least controversial of federal roles. In areas where private firms cannot expect to capture the full benefit of their investment, R&D tends to be underfunded. Where states and localities have only limited RD&D management expertise, the federal government is the obvious source of support for R&D activities. This is true for education.

There is little need for additional R&D on hardware or software products that have substantial application outside of education. The suppliers of such software and hardware products have every incentive to make R&D investments themselves. However, there are some needs, specifically related to education, for which school demand does not currently seem adequate to justify private investment or for which the short time horizons of public officials do not lead to state and local investment.

Areas of research and development that have particular benefits include the following:

1. Development of improved models for training teachers (and other staff) as well as better methods for promoting their professional development after graduation. Interactive network and CD-ROM applications could provide more timely and relevant sources of information and assistance than can be provided with current institutional arrangements.

2. Research and demonstration of ways in which to promote equal access to educational technology by all citizens.

3. Initial development of content software serving important educational needs, particularly in middle and secondary schools where market incentives appear inadequate to generate a sufficient supply.

4. Development of new assessment methods and instruments appropriate to the new learning outcomes sought by society and encouraged by the use of educational technology.

5. Development of advanced software tools that ease the creation of applications or the use of networks.

6. Continued work on learning and cognitive science.

7. Demonstration and assessment of effective technology-enabled learning processes.

We believe effectively planned and well-run demonstrations can produce high-quality information concerning the potential of technology for the improvement of learning. Demonstration projects also provide a means for the federal government to share some of the risks associated with new ventures. Solicitations associated with such programs provide the opportunity to stimulate the development of effective new technology applications. Support for demonstrations, if properly structured, can also help develop new sources of assistance to schools and teachers. The Technology Challenge Grant Program, sponsored by the Department of Education, has been put in place to help promote these objectives.

The federal actions proposed here are comparatively modest but of considerable importance. We expect them to provide guidance to the rapid development and deployment of educational technology that is now taking place. The key common quality of all the activities is that they provide information that will help educators, business people, parents, and policymakers contribute more effectively to this deployment.

The nation's most important educational goal must be to produce learners adequately prepared for life and work in the 21st century. Faced by uncertain demands, we should ensure that our youth master basic language and mathematics skills (perhaps in the context of studying subjects like history and science). But it is important that they also learn how to gather information and collaborate with others in the use of that information in solving problems and making informed judgments on public and private concerns. The nation must develop schools that can enable our youth to meet these goals. Properly employed, educational technology will make a major contribution to those schools and their students.

ACKNOWLEDGMENTS

Many people have contributed to our efforts. Linda Roberts, head of the Office of Technology at the U.S. Department of Education and Ed Fitzsimmons of the Office of Science and Technology Policy provided continuing advice and encouragement in their roles as sponsors of our work. Jonathan Hoyt and Gwen Solomon (Office of Educational Technology), Dexter Fletcher (Institute for Defense Analysis), and Gary Bridgewater (Office of Science and Technology Policy) provided encouragement and support throughout.

We owe a large debt of thanks to the individuals who took the time to participate in our workshops; their names are listed in the appendix. A number of them took the time to follow up their participation with notes and additional input. In addition, many people in government and industry took the time to talk with us; we appreciate their contributions of insights and data. Within RAND, Brent Keltner, David McArthur, Douglas Merrill, Sue Purnell, and Randy Ross made important contributions through their writing and advice. Karl Sun was responsible for the research on school district investment reported in Chapter Four. Nancy Rizor competently handled the logistics of the workshops. Jim Harvey regularly provided valuable advice and counsel as well as writing grace. Finally, Wally Baer (RAND) and Larry Frase (Educational Testing Service) provided cogent and useful comments on an earlier draft of this report.

Obviously, errors in fact and judgment are solely the responsibility of the authors.

Chapter One

INTRODUCTION

In 1994, public elementary and secondary schools spent approximately $3 billion to purchase educational technology.[1] Additional funds were spent on video equipment and telephones lines and for training school staff. President Clinton, Vice President Gore, and Secretary of Education Riley have called for all schools to be connected to the national information infrastructure (NII) by the year 2000. New federal legislation, such as the Goals 2000: Educate America Act, gives educational technology a prominent position. The reauthorized Elementary and Secondary Education Act (now called the Improving America's Schools Act (IASA)) gives technology prominent mention with separate legislation (Title III) and the requirement that the Department of Education (DoED) prepare a national plan to promote the use of technology. Across the country, telephone and cable companies are talking about wiring schools, and state public utility commissions are considering how to ensure universal access. Sales of education-like "edutainment" software to the home, while still modest, grew dramatically in 1994. A revolution in schooling, induced by the extraordinary advances in information technology that is comparable to that seen in industry and commerce, may be under way.

Despite all this activity, however, examples of schoolwide use of technology are comparatively rare and isolated. Use of technology in instruction tends to be by individual teachers. Few schools as a whole have embraced technology and used it to transform the con-

---

[1]We elaborate on this estimate in Chapter Three.

tent and mode of instruction. Evidence that technology can enable instructional practices that yield significantly improved outcomes or that promise greater efficiency in schooling is sparse. While parents strongly support introducing technology into schools, this support seems to reflect a belief that skill in the use of computers and telecommunications is key to success in the workplace rather than that such technology can lead to fundamentally improved schooling.

Funding is said to be a problem. Some communities have succeeded in passing special levies to support acquisition of technology, and a few states have appropriated funds to help schools connect to telecommunications services. More than a few teachers have purchased computers and software themselves to use in their classrooms. However, when schools are urged to modernize by reformers, business people, parents, or policymakers, teachers and administrators complain that they simply do not have the resources needed to acquire and learn to use technology in schools.

This report examines the issues surrounding the growing school acquisition and use of modern information technology. Its goal is to provide a base of information that will inform policymakers and others who are seeking strategies by which the nation can effectively use modern technologies to improve learning in classrooms, schools, and homes. The emphasis on educational improvement is the central organizing principle of this report. We certainly believe that all students in the modern world should possess at least basic abilities to use computers and telecommunications services. We also believe that such objectives will be easily achieved as both networks and computers become more ubiquitous. The more difficult question is whether technology, suitably implemented, has the potential to enable schools, students, and parents to make a significant improvement in the level and relevance of learning.

Thus, inevitably, policies related to technology become intertwined with the larger national efforts now under way to reform and restructure our schools. Components of these efforts include

- the state-level planning taking place under Goals 2000
- numerous state and local efforts to develop clearer educational standards and restructure school operations

- the effort of the New American Schools Development Corporation and others to create and implement new school designs

- major initiatives such as the New Standards Project to develop assessments that better reflect the knowledge and skills required by citizens in today's world

- higher education's emerging activities to improve the preparation of people for teaching in elementary and secondary schools

- the national efforts to raise standards for teacher certification.

Thus we are concerned with how technology can help advance the common goal of these efforts, and, in turn, how these efforts can advance the effective educational application of technology. Since we will generally be concerned with national strategies, our major emphasis is to inform decisionmaking in the federal government.

EDUCATIONAL TECHNOLOGY DEFINED

Policymakers and the public often pose questions concerning the effectiveness and cost of technology in education, implying that technology is, in itself, an educational activity. In fact, as in business, technology in education is a tool; a means to an end with endless specific implementation possibilities. A computer can serve as a freestanding or networked workstation that provides tutoring to a student and can be structured to adapt to his or her responses. It can serve as a word processor or to support desktop publishing for reporting the work of students, for example, in carrying out a multidisciplinary project on the history of a region or community. Electronic mail (E-mail) or voice mail systems can facilitate communications between parents and teachers or among students. The possibilities are endless, and the message is that the simple question "how effective is technology-supported education?" is essentially unanswerable because of the many ways in which technology can be used.

Table 1.1 suggests some of the numerous potential uses of technology in educational settings. What is striking about this list is its similarity to lists that can be constructed for uses in many workplaces. Computers and telecommunications technology, in general, have substituted for (and usually improved upon) much of the routine

Table 1.1

Some Examples of the Use of Technology in Support of Elementary and Secondary Education

Type of Educational Activity	Examples of Technology Use
Support for individual learning activities	Stand-alone drill and practice units for particular skills
	CD-ROM- or Internet-accessed resource bases
	Assistance in searching for information
	Communication with experts
	Computational and writing tools (word processors and spreadsheets)
	Simulations that help visualize systems or mathematical or scientific concepts
Support for group learning activities	E-mail supporting group communication
	Presentational software to allow group to collaborate on presentation
	Video to support presentation of community-based projects
	Communication allowing collaboration among schools for collection and analysis of data
Support for instructional management	Integration of curriculum, standards, and assessments
	Management of student portfolios and exhibitions
	Support for development of individual student instructional plans or contracts
Communications	Communication for remote locations (such as rural schools) that permit access to expertise, resources, and improved learning environments
	Improved communication among students, teachers, and parents
Administrative functions	Support for attendance, accountability functions, and other administrative activities

communication in a workplace. They have provided enormously improved tools for analysis of data and for presentation of those analyses by a significantly widened group of workers. They are changing the manner in which information is delivered to customers and clients in the workplace. For many educational tasks, technologies play analogous roles to those of the workplace.

There have been many efforts through the years to introduce technology into the classroom. In the 1960s and 70s, a strong effort was made to introduce instructional television into classrooms across the nation. Generally, the vision of individuals and organizations that promoted educational television failed to be achieved, and there is little evidence that educational television made much of an impact upon the typical school. It failed to alter the structure of instruction in fundamental and positive ways. But if it did not have the wide-scale impact originally envisioned, it cannot be said to have had no impact. Few teachers today would want to do without access to television and, more important, the VCR, which allows him or her to introduce a quality and quantity of informational resources to a class that far exceeds that available by filmstrips and 16 millimeter film. Perhaps more important, television and telecommunications have made rich instructional experiences available to remote and sparsely populated areas that previously had no opportunity to access them.

The first extensive uses of computers in schools took the form of support for individual learning activities. These provided drill and practice for individual students and, as they were developed and refined, came to include extensive instructional management features that helped to guide students through extensive bodies of instructional material. Modern versions of these systems, known as integrated learning systems (ILSs), are found in about 30 percent of the nation's schools and have found widespread use in programs for the educationally disadvantaged and for remedial instruction.[2]

These large educational systems often span several years of curriculums and were originally sold with associated hardware and networking. Because of the system's cost—upwards of $30,000—each is

---

[2]Many modern educational technology advocates view the ILS with disdain. While currently the largest single component of educational software in the schools, the ILS is seen as difficult to integrate into the activities of the school as a whole and inconsistent with the type of instruction that these advocates seek. It is also, in retrospect, seen as absorbing resources that could be more effectively used in a decentralized system. Our view is more tolerant: The ILS is simply one of many tools that can be used (or misused) in instructional settings. For a discussion of these issues see Newman, 1994

generally sold directly to central offices that procured them on behalf of schools within a district. Teachers frequently participated in the system's selection, and training for teachers was (and is) usually an important component of the purchase.

In many ways, these systems are reminiscent of the time-shared computer systems that were introduced into workplaces in the late 1960s and early 1970s. While offering enormous potential for delivering services to workers or students, they were costly and rigid by today's standards. The continued rapid decline in the cost of computational power and mass storage soon allowed the introduction of the personal computer and the independence and autonomy that is associated with it. A whole new market for software that catered to individual needs and enthusiasms began to appear, and information systems managers began to lose their control over the manner in which computational technology was used in the workplace.

Left unchecked, the growth of autonomous computing might have introduced disparate computational and writing aids in the work-place but might not have led to fundamental changes. However, these computers were soon linked with one another and client servers in immensely flexible ways. Many workers could access databases. Networks began to serve as substitutes for intra- and inter-office memos, or as proprietary networks, and then the Internet emerged, with clients and suppliers in distant locations. Decentralized computing power coupled with effective software and networks vastly enhanced the ability of "frontline" workers to acquire, analyze, and use information. Considerable restructuring of the workplace was possible and desirable in the interest of greater effectiveness and efficiency. Indeed, in many cases, existing patterns of organizational behavior were undermined and forced to restructure.

The same qualities of computing and telecommunications equipment and service that made it possible to restructure the workplace make it possible to restructure and reengineer the workplace called school. Technology allows students or teachers to perform traditional tasks with a speed and quality that were not easily attainable in the past. It allows individual students and teachers to work both individually and collaboratively. Connected to the nation's information infrastructure, it provides access to fellow teachers and students as well as a vast store of information that is increasingly available on-line. Technology provides the possibility for massive shifts in the ways in which students, teachers, and administrators use their time and for new and better forms of accountability to parents and the community. This is the message behind the examples in Table 1.1. Technology is no longer found in the form of a few well-developed tools to be introduced more or less intact into schools but in a whole raft of capabilities that can serve the ends of teaching and learning. And, as has been the case in many businesses, introducing information technology into the schools may provide the catalyst that enables and forces the restructuring necessary to meet our national education goals.

WHY IS EDUCATIONAL TECHNOLOGY AN IMPORTANT COMPONENT OF PUBLIC POLICY?

The incentives inherent in a competitive marketplace that have driven the restructuring of business are largely missing in public elementary and secondary education. Because of these differences in incentives and because, in most instances, elementary and secondary education is provided by the state, explicit public actions are required to more fully realize the potential benefits of technology in education.

The improvement of the effectiveness, efficiency, and equality of opportunity in public education has been an important object of federal and state policy for many decades. In the mid-1980s, *A Nation at Risk*[3] forcefully argued that the United States needed an improved education system to survive and prosper in a world that was increasingly competitive and interdependent. States and localities moved to increase the quality and rigor of elementary and secondary education, but with results that continued to be found inadequate.

The perception that these reform efforts had failed to achieve the desired level of improvement led the nation's state governors and the president to establish a set of national goals to guide local, state, and

---

[3]National Commission on Excellence in Education, 1983.

federal efforts. These goals were subsequently amended and made a part of federal law by the Congress in the Goals 2000 legislation.

Technology can clearly assist schools, and the nation generally, to more effectively meet many of the goals contained in the legislation. Perhaps most important is the goal that calls for *all* students to possess demonstrated competency in challenging subject matter and be prepared for productive citizenship, continued learning, and productive employment. Because all students do not learn at the same rate or respond effectively to the same styles of instruction, educators have for years called for tailoring educational methods to learner needs and abilities to deal with these differences. This ideal has not often been reached. Most teachers and schools have, instead, tended to provide a common program of instruction for all students with some enrichment for the fastest learners and some remedial attention for the slowest. Tracking students, explicitly or implicitly, has also provided a crude form of individualization by allowing students of differing skills and interests to be grouped so that a common curriculum and instructional strategy can be developed for these groups. While popular with parents, particularly parents of the better students, tracking has been widely attacked for failing to meet the educational needs of many other groups of students and thus as inconsistent with the vision that all students should master challenging subject matter and skills.

Educational technology can make an important contribution to the ideal of tailoring education methods more closely to individual learner needs and abilities. It can provide additional specialized tutoring to those that need more time to master a subject area, both in and outside of school. It can create learning environments that engage large groups of students, freeing teachers for more intensive work with other small groups of students with common interests or needs. It can provide enrichment and extended learning opportunities to students who have mastered the core subject area and are anxious to move on to more challenging material. Perhaps most important, technology can provide the instructional management systems to support individual student educational programs by allowing teachers to guide the student's learning activities and keep track of the student's mastery of subject matter.

Technology can and clearly does contribute to other national education goals as well, including the support of life-long learning, the professional development of teachers, and the achievement of high proficiency in science. But while technology can clearly serve these instrumental purposes, it is also important to recognize the role technology can play in breaking down traditional bureaucratic schools and school systems, thereby fomenting productive change. This opportunity was clearly articulated by Louis V. Gerstner, Jr. Chairman and CEO of IBM, in a speech to the National Governors' Association. After calling for higher and more meaningful standards, an increased focus on investment, and greater use of technology, he said,

> [I]nformation technology is the fundamental underpinning of the science of structural re-engineering. It is the force that revolutionizes business, streamlines government and enables instant communications and the exchange of information among people and institutions around the world.

> But information technology has not made even its barest appearance in most public schools. Look around. The most visible forms of technology remain the unintelligible public address systems, which serve largely to interrupt the business of learning, and the copier in the principal's office, which spews out the forms and regulations that are the life blood of the education bureaucracy.

> Before we can get the education revolution rolling, we need to recognize that our public schools are low-tech institutions in a high-tech society. The same changes that have brought cataclysmic change to every facet of business can improve the way we teach students and teachers. And it can also improve the efficiency and effectiveness of how we run our schools.[4]

We share Gerstner's sense of the potential importance that technology has for the improvement of American education. However, realizing that potential comes at a cost. Both the potential and the cost are explored in this report.

---

[4]Gerstner, 1995.

RESEARCH APPROACH AND OUTLINE OF REPORT

To address the potential, costs, and challenges associated with increasing the level of technology in the nation's schools, RAND's Critical Technologies Institute (CTI) convened five two-day workshops. These workshops dealt with

- the professional development of teachers—both the development that is needed to realize the benefits of technology and the opportunities that technology presents for assisting teachers and administrative staff with their own professional growth

- issues in the planning and financing of educational technology and infrastructure in elementary and secondary schools

- the nature of the market for educational software (two workshops)

- what is known about the success of technology-rich schools in dealing with a wide spectrum of students.[5]

In addition, we commissioned analyses from colleagues at RAND and elsewhere. These dealt with the costs of technology in technology-rich schools, the effectiveness of technology-enabled programs, and the desirable attributes of wide-area networks supporting technology in schools. We have also benefited from monitoring the active network discussions organized around the subjects of our workshops and the testimony of experts at a series of regional hearings, both of which were organized and conducted by the federal Department of Education. A report on teachers and technology prepared by the Office of Technology Assessment (OTA) has also provided valuable input.[6]

In Chapter Two of this report, we review what is known about the current use of technology in education. Drawing on several national surveys and papers prepared for OTA, we describe the current use of technology in schools in quite broad terms. The picture is of rapid but uneven growth in the use of technology over the past decade. We

---

[5]Summaries of each of these workshops are available separately. Participants are listed in the appendix.

[6]U.S. Congress, 1995.

also describe a sample of pioneer schools nominated by experts and compare them with the broader national picture. The amount of technology and the uses to which it is put in these pioneer schools stand in marked contrast to the typical school that is described by the national data. Moreover, the testimony of both participants in and observers of these schools suggests excitement and high performance.

We conclude this chapter with a review of what we know about the effectiveness of educational activities and schools as a whole when they are supported by extensive technology. Obviously, with the rapid development of new applications of technology, much remains to be learned about the effectiveness of technology-enabled instruction and schools. However, we judge the evidence shows that, properly implemented, such instruction and schools show great promise.

In Chapter Three we turn to an examination of what we know about the costs of technology in schools. The rapidity with which technology is changing and its use is evolving makes pinning down these costs quite difficult. Using data from several sources, we estimate the existing expenditures for educational technology. We then go on to create a range of costs for schools with ubiquitous computing, telecommunications, and video support. We base these estimates on the small sample of schools mentioned above.

The bottom line is that if all schools had technology-enabled environments similar to schools in the midrange of those we examined, the costs would be on the order of 5 percent of total current expenditures for K–12 education. While this cost seems modest—it is well below the proportions for many service businesses—it is four times the estimated current level of K–12 expenditures for technology.

In Chapter Four, we consider three national, systemic challenges to the widespread adoption and effective implementation of technology in the schools:

1. Financing the costs of acquiring and developing the capability to use educational technology.

2. Enabling teachers to develop the capabilities required to function effectively in new pedagogical environments.

3. Creating the software that is needed to realize the full potential of technology-enabled schooling.

Concerning financing, we conclude that a plausible educational infrastructure can be put in place and maintained in schools for a level of funding approximating 3 to 5 percent of the total cost of public elementary and secondary education in the nation. This is a national average, and it represents an annualized cost rather than distinct estimates of investment and continued operating costs.

The individual school or school district faces the additional challenge associated with the peculiarities of school finance. While the steady state, annualized costs of technology may not be overwhelming, the schools need to make sizable initial investments in equipment, renovations, and training; investments that are large relative to current school budgets. Unfortunately, schools do not have an "investment mentality" nor, frequently, the access to financing mechanisms that enable them to deal with this problem. Moreover, the political milieu that schools find themselves in makes targeted investment very difficult.[7]

To finance these expenditures, either significant restructuring of school budgets is required or the public will have to agree to increased levels of spending. In either case, educational leaders, policymakers, and the public will no doubt continue to want evidence that the use of technology will lead to more effective (and perhaps more cost-effective) schools.

The second barrier poses an equally difficult challenge. Most teachers now in classrooms have had little formal instruction on how to

---

[7]As with the development of teachers' skills, this problem is not really restricted to technology. The transformation and restructuring of a school requires incremental resources. RAND's work for the New American Schools Development Corporation suggests that increments in funding of perhaps 10 percent annually over a two to three year period may be required for transformations that do not necessarily have high technology content. There are many indications that school systems find it enormously difficult to marshal resources to make such investments in a few schools. Instead, schools are implored to restructure themselves, often with the "sweat equity" of their staffs.

use technology or on how to teach in the sorts of learning environments made feasible by technology. Even new teachers have received little training in these areas from their colleges and universities. Developing capabilities to make effective use of technology is a major task for education policymakers.[8]

The third barrier concerns the development of content software for use in schools. The nature of the market for content materials in elementary and secondary education has been shaped by decades of interaction between textbook manufacturers and school systems. The market is shaped by adoption practices, often set by law, and by the ways in which school budgets for materials are allocated and committed. While a burgeoning educational software industry is developing, it is largely independent of traditional content providers with their large sales forces and finds marketing its products to schools a daunting and unrewarding task.

In Chapter Five, we draw out of our analysis a set of broad findings. With these as background, we suggest a number of strategic principles that should govern the nation's efforts to bring technology to the schools. We conclude with recommended actions by the federal government.

---

[8]The problem of teacher competency *is not* primarily related to technology but rather to the larger issues of content knowledge and classroom management skills required by pedagogical strategies dealing with the individual needs of students.

Chapter Two

THE USE AND EFFECTIVENESS OF EDUCATIONAL TECHNOLOGY TODAY

This chapter broadly describes the current use of technology to improve school effectiveness and student learning. We begin by summarizing current capacity and usage data for the nation's schools. Then, drawing on the experience of selected technology-rich schools, we suggest a vision of what widespread use of technology in schools might look like. Finally, we summarize evidence related to effectiveness. This chapter provides the backdrop for considering the costs and challenges for achieving more effective and widespread use of technology, the subjects of Chapters Three and Four.

CURRENT SCHOOL AND STUDENT USE OF TECHNOLOGY

This subsection draws heavily on a few surveys that have sought to characterize the penetration and use of computer and communication technologies in schools. The picture that emerges is one of a fairly rapid increase in school capacity, but it is also clear that average student use is still very limited.

Existing Penetration of Technology in Schools

Technology is penetrating the nation's schools. One of the simplest measures is computer "density." Figure 2.1 shows that density, measured by the number of students per computer, has fallen rather dramatically in the past 12 years. This growth has been promoted by declines in the costs of computing power, improvements in the quality of productivity software, and the belief of increasing numbers

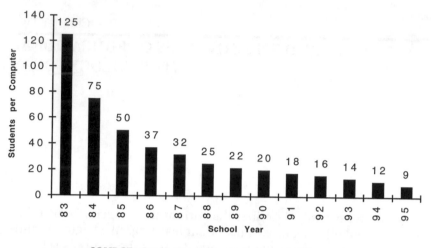

SOURCE: Quality Education Data, Inc. (QED), 1994.

**Figure 2.1—Decline in Number of Students Per Computer
in Public K–12 Schools, 1983–84 to 1995–96**

of parents that a capability to use technology constitutes another basic skill that schools should provide their students.

These data suggest that schools across the country are making significant progress in acquiring technological capacity. However, this simple representation hides important features of and differences among districts and schools. For example, the rapid introduction of computers in the mid and late 1980s suggests that many school computers are relatively old. At the beginning of school year 1993–94, nearly half of the computers in schools were early model Apple computers.[1] Many of the Apple Macintosh and IBM clones lack hard drives and the capability to use the Internet and the new multimedia technology that is rapidly becoming available. These computers may provide reasonable platforms for learning keyboard skills or for using

---

[1]QED, 1994, p. 21. QED's data are collected from all schools. The data are reported for the situation as of the beginning of the school year, and if responses are not received in time for the publication, older data are used. Henry Becker, who has used the database and consulted with QED, suggests that in recent years, the data may understate the numbers of computers in use during the school year by 25 percent. See p. 8 of the QED report and Becker, 1994.

older drill-and-practice software, but they are unable to run most more recently developed software.[2]

The penetration of computers varies by the size and grade level of schools. Table 2.1 provides data for 1993–94. In general, small schools are better equipped than large schools, while secondary schools are better equipped than elementary schools.

Confounding these average differences in computer density is the reality that there are early adopters and enthusiasts of any innovation, so that some (pioneer) schools can be expected to have much higher densities of computers and, very likely, to use them in different ways. The Quality Education Data (QED) census provides some hints of this phenomenon in data shown in Table 2.2.

These data suggest that in the fall of 1994, only 3 percent of the nation's K–12 students were in schools that had at least one computer for every five students, a density that those advocating the benefits of technology-intensive schools judge barely adequate. A simple calculation is revealing. With perfect maintenance and scheduling, one computer for every five students would provide 30 minutes a day of computer time per student in a five-hour school day.

Table 2.1

Number of Students Per Computer, by School Size and Level, 1993–94

Grade Level	School Enrollment			Total
	1–299	300–749	750+	
Elementary	12	16	20	16
Middle/Jr. High	10	12	14	13
Senior High	7	10	12	11
All Schools	10	14	15	14

NOTE: Adapted from QED, 1994, p. 15.

---

[2]Using somewhat older data, Becker estimates that in addition to the limitations of the 8-bit technology used by old Apple machines, fully 80 percent of school computers lack hard drives and a connection to local-area networks. Becker, 1994, p. 68.

Table 2.2

Variations in the Penetration of Computers Among Schools, Fall 1994

Students Per Computer	Schools		Students (millions)		Average No. of Students per Computer
Fewer than 5	3,433	(4%)	1.2	(3%)	3.9
Between 5 and 12.4	36,256	(44%)	18.1	(41%)	8.9
Between 12.5 and 23	35,355	(43%)	20.1	(46%)	16.5
More than 23	7,703	(9%)	4.4	(10%)	28.5

NOTE: QED, 1994. Adapted from table in undated paper by Jeanne Hayes and Dennis L. Bybee, "Toward Defining the 'Greatest Need for Educational Technology.'" The paper was prepared to support congressional testimony in March 1995.

Many are concerned that this distribution of computer penetration in schools is highly correlated with the resources available in a district or with the characteristics of the students that are served by a school. Is the number of students per computer higher in poor schools or in schools serving one or another special population? The answer appears to be yes to both, but not by much. Using data from the International Education Association's (IEA) survey of schools in 1992, Becker notes

> Compared to the differences in computer access between students in small and large schools, the disparities among regions, types of communities, and schools attended by different ethnic and socioeconomic groups are relatively small.[3]

He finds students in cities with populations over 200,000, and Hispanic students somewhat disadvantaged. His analysis of the QED data for the same time period shows that the average black student attended a school with 4 percent fewer computers per student (a lower density) than that of the average white student. Hispanic students fared worse; on the average they were in schools with 13 percent fewer computers per student than whites.[4]

---

[3]Becker, 1994, p. 51.

[4]Note that Becker has adopted the more traditional definition of density, the number of computers per student.

Becker notes an interesting finding that reveals the indirect importance of federal policies in influencing technology in the schools. For the 1992 school year, which the IEA study surveyed, elementary schools with more than a quarter of their students eligible for Chapter I funding tended to have more computers per capita than elementary schools in general.[5] QED data were consistent with this finding, indicating that elementary schools with 50 percent or more Chapter I eligible students had 29 percent more computers per capita than the average elementary school. This helps explain statements by industry representatives attending the CTI software workshops that Chapter I schools play a major role in their marketing strategy.

In summary, these data show a continuing penetration of computers in the nation's schools but considerable variation among schools and districts. The combination of steady acquisition and accumulation of equipment by schools in a period of rapid technological change suggests that much of the school computer inventory is technologically obsolete although it may retain considerable educational usefulness. Overall, while the rate of penetration for schools serving minority and poverty populations is somewhat lower than average, the difference appears not to be extreme.

Use of Computers by Students

Data on capacity level do not necessarily provide much insight into how or how much the equipment is used. The IEA study does contain information provided by technology coordinators, teachers, and students about the nature and amount of computer use. The information is sketchy and sometimes contradictory but provides a few hints concerning student use in 1992. Table 2.3 is taken from Becker's analysis of data from computer coordinators concerning the percentage of student computer time devoted to various subjects.

These data suggest that, at least in high school, the use of computers is substantially in support of acquiring skills for work and further ed-

---

[5]Chapter I was the section of the Elementary and Secondary Education Act that provided supplemental funding to schools with high proportions of educationally disadvantaged students. In 1994, this act was significantly revised as the Improving America's Schools Act. The corresponding section is called Title I.

Table 2.3

**Estimated Percentage of Student Computer Time
Devoted to Different Subjects by School Level, 1992**

Subject	Elementary	Middle	High School
Computer education			
Word processing	12.5	15.6	15.0
Key boarding	15.0	14.1	12.5
Database, spreadsheets, tools	3.7	8.8	10.9
Computer programming	2.9	6.9	7.1
Subtotal: Computer education	*34.1*	*45.4*	*45.5*
Academic subjects			
Mathematics	18.3	11.0	7.7
English	16.6	10.5	7.4
Science	8.0	6.6	6.2
Social studies	8.4	5.6	4.1
Foreign languages	0.5	1.4	2.7
Fine arts	1.9	2.1	3.0
Subtotal: Academic subjects	*53.7*	*37.2*	*31.2*
Vocational subjects			
Business education	2.2	3.1	11.0
Industrial arts	0.5	3.7	6.4
Subtotal: Vocational subjects	*2.7*	*6.8*	*17.3*
Recreation and other			
Recreational use	8.8	9.5	6.0
Other	0.7	1.1	0.3
Subtotal: Recreation and other	*9.5*	*10.6*	*6.3*

SOURCE: Analysis of computer coordinator data from the 1992 IEA computers in education study (Table 4.1 in Becker, 1994).

ucation. About 63 percent of student computer time is devoted to computer education and vocational subjects; only 31 percent to the support of academic subjects. Not surprisingly, in elementary school, academic subjects account for a larger proportion of use.

One further issue about the nature of existing computer use deserves brief comment. Advocates for the increased student use of computer technology emphasize the potential for advancing the development of the student's "higher-order" thinking skills. Becker tried to distinguish activities like writing, analysis, and synthesis, which he believes are associated with developing such higher-order skills, from more routine skill- or fact-oriented learning. Using student data from the IEA survey, he develops statistics shown in Table 2.4.

At the elementary level, where many schools use computers for drill and practice, skills development predominates. At high schools, however, activities that mix skill development with the fostering of higher-order skills are more prominent.

The actual amount of time a student uses a computer is not easily estimated. Using data provided by technology coordinators, Becker makes a rough estimate that use might average 1.7 hours per student per week at elementary schools, 2.0 hours at middle schools, and 3.0 hours at high schools. However, he quickly goes on to note that data from student reports of their frequency of use suggest that "*few* students obtain the 'two hours per week' experience with computers that is the average per-student time estimated from the computer coordinator data."[6] In a later calculation, Becker suggests that the average use may be as little as a third of these estimates.[7]

Table 2.4

**Proportion of Student Activities That
Are Higher Order or Skill Development**

	Percentage of Student Activities		
Type of Use	Grade 5	Grade 8	Grade 11
Predominately higher order	4	10	14
Mixed skills and higher order	17	29	27
Predominately skill use	54	26	18
Little computer use	17	21	23
No use at all	9	14	20

SOURCE: Becker, 1994, Table 4.5.

Becker suggests that these student data provide a strong indication of the relatively infrequent use of computers in secondary school academic subjects.

---

[6]Becker, 1994, p. 32

[7]Becker, 1994, p. 35.

Most middle-school and high-school students report having used computers only once or twice during most of the school year (about 30 weeks). If we ignore truly occasional uses of computers and concentrate on those classes for which students used school computers on at least 10 occasions (i.e. once every 3 weeks), more than one-third of secondary school students reported using computers in a computer class, but only one student out of 11 reported having used school computers for an English class, one out of 15, for a math class, and only one out of 40, for a social studies or science class. Twice as many students even reported using computers for a business education class as for a social studies class even though only 30% of the students had a business class at all. When we consider that word processing is a major—probably *the* major activity—in secondary school computer education classes as well as in business education classes, it seems clear that school is still primarily a place to learn how to use word processing rather than a place to do word processing in order to achieve other academic goals. This is likely to even be more true of other applications such as spreadsheets and database programs, which have even been less integrated into subject-matter instructional practices than word processing.[8]

The picture painted by Becker for average student computer use in school in 1992 does not suggest that computers played a prominent role in their learning. He does note that the strongest predictor of student computer time is computer density, and that the trend toward higher density makes it more likely that student use will be directed to higher-order intellectual activities.[9] Thus, as the school computer inventory continues to rise and as more schools achieve densities comparable with those of schools currently in the top 10 percent or so, the amount and quality of student use would be expected to increase and improve.

Penetration of Telecommunication Networks

Comparatively few data exist on the school use of local or wide area networks. The explosive growth of Internet usage and the growth of other proprietary services such as America Online, Prodigy, and CompuServe hold considerable potential for education and educa-

---

[8]Becker, 1994, p. 71.
[9]Becker, 1994, p. 74.

tors. Wide area networks (WANs) can provide teachers and students with access to data and other resources far greater than what would typically be available locally. They provide the opportunity for students and teachers to collaborate widely with students and teachers at other schools, and to query experts and remote databases. They allow students to participate in scientific activities as they unfold (e.g., a NASA space experiment), which makes the learning experience more vivid and relevant. Indeed, a short "cruise" on either the Internet or one of the on-line services will quickly reveal numerous examples of these applications.

To discover the extent to which schools can currently access such networks, the U.S. Departments of Education and Commerce commissioned a study to gather data from a representative sample of schools in the fall of 1994. The analysis indicated that

> While 75 percent of public schools have access to some kind of computer network, only 49 percent have access to a wide area network—35 percent of public schools have access to the Internet and 14 percent have access to other wide area networks (e.g. CompuServe, America Online, Prodigy).[10]

Access to WANs varies by schooling level, too. Nearly half of the nation's secondary schools (49 percent) had access to the Internet, but only 30 percent of elementary schools. Mostly, the connections appear to be to a single point in the school, such as the media center or an administrative office. The data suggest that only 3 percent of school instructional space (i.e., classrooms, labs, and media centers) are directly connected to a WAN. For those who believe access to WANs should be seamlessly available to all students while learning, this figure is discouragingly low.

If access to WANs is to be widespread in the school building, local area networks (LANs) must exist. In recent years, the growth of such networks has been rapid. According to QED, 1994, 5 percent of public schools used LANs for instruction in 1991–92. Two years later, the number had more than doubled to 23 percent. Again the figures differ for high schools and elementary schools; 42 percent of high

---

[10]National Center for Education Statistics, 1995a, p. 3.

schools used LANs for instruction while only 17 percent of elementary schools did.[11] The growth in the number of school LANs appears to mirror the increase in computer density and prefigures the increase in access to WANs.

EXPERIENCE OF A HANDFUL OF TECHNOLOGY-RICH SCHOOLS

The average picture that we have just painted does not represent the leading edge in either school technology capacity or application. To improve our understanding of the educational potential of school technology, we turned to a handful of technology-rich schools where technology is not a marginal addition—curriculum and instruction have been changed, and the school day is reorganized to make effective use of technology.

To acquire this information, we convened a two-day workshop, inviting participation by representatives of five schools, which consultations with experts across the country confirmed were outstanding examples of the use of technology to support the school's educational mission. These schools are listed and briefly described in Table 2.5.

We consciously sought schools that served a variety of populations, revealed by the data in column 2 of Table 2.5. We aimed for geographic diversity and for representation among the different levels of K–12 education. To learn about technology and technology-related resources used, we surveyed each school independently for this information.[12] At the workshop, each representative presented evidence on school effectiveness and student learning. The following vignettes describe each school's technology program.

Blackstock Junior High School, Port Hueneme, California

With annual per-student expenditures in 1994 of $4,060 for some 960 students, many eligible for Chapter I support, this 36-classroom

---

[11]QED, 1994, p. 77.

[12]These are documented in Keltner and Ross, 1996.

school caters to a largely minority population of mostly Hispanic descent, with smaller numbers of Chinese and Vietnamese students. Twenty-two percent of the student body are characterized as having limited English-language skills. Keltner and Ross, 1996, describe the school as follows:

> Blackstock's model of educational technology delivery centers on creating what are called "smart classrooms." There are at present eight smart classrooms, including two for instruction in 7th grade science, one for instruction in 8th grade science, two for literature and history, one for ESL instruction, one for instruction in business education, and one called the Tech Lab 2000.[13] Each has been conceived and designed to support a technologically intensive educational delivery.
>
> The Tech Lab 2000 is perhaps most appropriately described as the futuristic equivalent of a wood or metal shop. Designed to make students familiar with the technology present in the modern workplace, the Tech Lab is outfitted with Computer Assisted Design (CAD) software, a Computer Numerically Controlled (CNC) flexible manufacturing system, pneumatic equipment, and a satellite dish. All of the other smart classrooms have between 25–30 computers on a local area network (LAN). Each is also equipped with a sophisticated file server and a SOTA switch to give the teacher maximum control over classroom dynamics. Students can all be working on the same project, e.g., a software program or an interactive video presentation, or there can be a variety of things going on in the classroom at the same time.
>
> There is also plenty of technology outside of the classrooms. In each of the schools' other classrooms, there are banks of ten computers and two printers. Teachers in the non-smart classrooms do not have the same sophisticated management system to control technology delivery, but are able to use many of the basic and important software applications, from word processing to interactive programs, in their instruction. They can also draw on the school's connection to the Internet to create a more technologically rich environment.

---

[13]A mathematics-smart classroom, nearly completed, will bring the total to nine.

Staff development efforts for teachers in the smart classrooms have centered on giving individual instructors large amounts of paid time-off to familiarize themselves with technology and to organize a technology-based curriculum. Of the eight teachers in the smart classrooms, four took a year off and one took two years off to prepare themselves. The other three teachers were given three weeks during the summer to prepare. In the latter cases, the teachers were setting up a second smart class in a subject area where one already existed. The presence of a teacher with technological and curricular know-how made it easier for the new teacher to get up and running more quickly. Ongoing staff development for all teachers, those in smart and non-smart classrooms alike, is supported by four paid days of technology training per year and a considerable amount of informal networking.

Up to the present, Blackstock has not had a technology coordinator to support staff development efforts, relying instead on paid leave time and informal networking. To keep the technology program running smoothly, there is a teacher who has devoted about a quarter of his time to technology-related problem-solving and to computer repairs. Starting next year this teacher will move into the position of full-time technology coordinator.

Christopher Columbus Middle School, Union City, New Jersey

Christopher Columbus (CC) is a small 7th and 8th grade school of 310 students in Union City, NJ. Reflecting the school district's student population, the largest number of CC's students are Hispanic. Many do not speak English at home, are enrolled in the English as a Second Language (ESL) program, and are eligible for free or reduced cost lunch in school. The school's program was developed with the guidance of a districtwide effort to reform curriculum and instruction. A "whole language philosophy of education," a project-based rather than textbook-based approach to curriculum and instruction, and a reorganization of the school day into a smaller number of larger time blocks are the basis for CC's technology implementation. It has had particular assistance from the local telephone company, which has viewed it as an important test site for a program to enhance communications with the home. Keltner and Ross describe it as follows:

Technology has been used to create a "research-based" curriculum. The school's curriculum integrates traditional subject areas, but has as its main focus an emphasis on teaching students 'how to learn." Students are encouraged to become active learners through the use of structured research activities and group project work. To facilitate the transition to a student-centered learning environment, instructional delivery at the school[14] has been reorganized. Rather than the traditional 50-minute period, classes meet for between one-and-one-half hours and two hours. The longer class periods allow students to delve deeper into their course work and give teachers more time to act as educational facilitators.

Each of the school's twelve classrooms is outfitted with five computers (a mix of Macs and PCs), a printer, and a video presentation station (VCR, laserdisk player and presentation monitors). There are 30 additional Macintosh computers with CD-ROM capabilities in the school's central computer lab. To allow students to experiment with multimedia production, the computer lab is also outfitted with camcorders, a video projector, and a computer video editing unit. The school has two LANs, one for Macs, the other for PCs. The PCs are linked to the Internet to allow remote resources to be integrated into classroom instruction.

To get CC's technology program up and running, each of the school's 15 teachers were given six days training in each of the first two years of implementation. After the two-year start-up period, staff development continued at a lower level of intensity, with each teacher receiving an average of three days of paid on-going training per year. To keep the school's technology program running smoothly, there is a full-time technology coordinator on-site. The technology coordinator is responsible for conducting student computer classes, supporting teachers, and making technology repairs.

---

[14]Bell Atlantic has worked with the Christopher Columbus Middle School over the past two years to add a high-speed school-and-home computer-communications network to the school technology program. The network involves the use of high-speed telephone lines (ISDN) to connect school computers and 150 student and teacher homes to a library of CD-ROM and software titles stored centrally on six file servers at a Bell Atlantic site. This component of the CC technology program remains experimental and is not described further here.

East Bakersfield High School, Bakersfield, California

East Bakersfield High School emphasizes a technology-rich, school-to-work transition program in a school serving 2,400 students, with a majority Latino population and an educational philosophy that education equals experience. The following is from Keltner and Ross, 1996:

> The school's chief administrator aims to have students understand early that their high school education shapes their job prospects, and that their present educational experience is a way of building job-relevant skills. Exposure to business and career-oriented themes begins immediately in the ninth grade and continues throughout their high school education, and includes resume writing, portfolio building and project activities oriented towards the local business community.

> The school's curriculum is organized around five career "tracks". The career tracks are not targeted at specific ability levels, nor do they consist of a core set of classes that each pupil must complete. Rather, they are designed to allow students to develop technical and applied skills related to broad industry groups. One career track is oriented around course work in science, technology, engineering and manufacturing (STEM). Included in this curriculum is everything from a freshman class in the principles of technology to advance placement physics for seniors. Students in this career track can make use of the Hands on Science & Technology (HOST) Center to use technology in the design and fabrication of exhibits. A second career track prepares students for employment in health-care. The school's health careers academy has 200 professional partners throughout the Bakersfield area, which offer students internships during the school year and the summer break. A third career track is Communications and Graphics and Arts. Courses in this track include forensics, writing and a yearbook class.

> Another career track is known as human and government services, designed to prepare students for careers in teaching, law and public administration. Particular attention is given to developing strong skills in both written and oral communication. The remaining career track is oriented towards developing business and entrepreneurial skills. Students can participate in a one-semester class called EB enterprises, in which they carry out projects in a high-tech

office environment for teachers, school administrators or community businesses. Project work includes developing inventory programs, generating descriptions of courses and scholarships, and doing graphics for signs and brochures. Students alternate as office managers in order to learn how to manage tasks and coworkers.

Technology-based instruction is integrated smoothly into course work from beginning to end. As freshmen, students take a nine-week course in keyboarding and basic computer literacy. Writing assignments in the freshman English and history core courses are organized to ensure that all students moving into their sophomore year are proficient in the use of word processing programs. As seniors, students have to complete a technology-based project as a graduation requirement. Projects involve the use of computers, graphics software or video equipment.

General instruction between the first and final years is heavily technology-based. Math classes integrate an interactive math program. English, history and social studies teachers have access to writing labs as well as a large number of video towers equipped with CD-ROM, videodisk players and VCRs. The school building is in the process of being rewired to accommodate network technology. Next year, many of the classrooms will have Internet connectivity.

Administrators at E. Bakersfield use a variety of measures to support technology-related staff development. There is a limited amount of funding available for paid, formal technology training—the school's staff development budget allocates an average of one paid day per teacher per year. Much of this budget goes to training new teachers. New teachers without any prior training in computer technology are expected to spend several days during the summer break in training to achieve basic fluency. New teachers with more experience are typically requested to train on their own time. To support informal development efforts, the school has a teacher lab equipped with nine computers and a laser printer. Many of the computers have CD-ROM capabilities. To keep the technology component of the school running smoothly, the school also has a half-time technology coordinator, a full-time repair specialist and a budget for hiring network specialists on an as needed basis.

Northbrook Middle School, Houston, Texas

Northbrook Middle School is a new school that was created in an old building. It serves a 6th through 8th grade population of under 800 students drawn largely from families of Hispanic migrant workers. The school had an initial six million dollars for startup, of which one and a half million was devoted to technology. Keltner and Ross provide the following description:

> The school administrators understand their main mission to be the preparation of their students as life-long learners for the world of work. The school's curriculum, while centered on traditional academic subjects, places heavy emphasis on students acquiring critical thinking and problem solving skills. Teachers are expected to assist students in learning how to find and analyze information. To support this student-centered learning environment, the school is organized into four educational clusters. Teachers and students in each cluster work together to support one another in continually expanding their ability to gather information and solve problems. Technology is viewed as a primary vehicle to help students develop critical thinking and problem solving skills. Technology permits instruction to be tailored to individual student needs.

> Northbrook's technology program is centered primarily on the use of computers. With over 400 computers in place in the school's six technology labs and 48 classrooms, Northbrook has a student to computer ratio of just under 2:1. Each of the school's classrooms is outfitted with between five and six computers. All of the computers have built-in CD-ROM capabilities in order to expand the range of software products available for student use. Access to network resources are used to support student information searches. Computers in the classrooms, in the computer labs, and in the library are networked together in a school-wide LAN with Internet connectivity. Teachers also make use of multimedia presentation equipment. Each of the classrooms is outfitted with a videodisk player, a scanner and some multimedia editing equipment.

> To support the technology program, Northbrook has relied primarily on on-site staff development. Each of the school's 48 teachers received two weeks of technology-related staff development in the summer prior to the school start-up. On an ongoing basis, teachers participate on the average of three to four days of paid training each

year. Additional personnel to support the technology program include a full-time technology assistant and a part-time district technology coordinator. These two individuals are responsible for conducting in-house training and keeping the technology running smoothly.

Taylorsville Elementary School, Taylorsville, Indiana

The Taylorsville Elementary School serves a little over 600 suburban students in pre-K through 6th grade. The students are predominately from largely lower middle-class, white families. Keltner and Ross provide the following description:

> Taylorsville is one of several schools in Indiana working with the Modern Red School House (MRSH) educational design team—a New American School Development Corp. (NASDC) activity—to bring information technology into its educational delivery. The school's technology plan, its hardware layout, and its staff development effort reflect the essentials of the MRSH design. The most important role for technology in the school's educational design is to support a commitment to self-paced individualized learning.

> Taylorsville's curriculum emphasizes core subjects, aiming for high levels of proficiency in language arts, math, science, history and geography. Despite this emphasis on standardization in content, educational delivery focuses on students proceeding through course work at their own pace. Instructional strategies promote multi-age, multi-year groupings and stress team-based project work. The opportunities for regrouping teams during project work allow individual students to develop their skills in different areas at an appropriate speed. By virtue of their role in integrating instruction across subjects and grades, teachers play a key role in facilitating the transition to a self-paced student environment.

> The school's technology plan provides students with plentiful access to networked computers. Taylorsville has one computer lab equipped with 25 Apple computers. Each of the school's 25 classrooms has a cluster of four student computers, one teacher computer, and a printer. Some of the classroom computers have internal CD-ROM drives to increase the range of software applications accessible to students. A school-wide LAN connects classroom computers to the computer lab and to administrative offices. At

present, students can access the Internet from two computers in the library media center. Plans provide for Internet connectivity to each classroom. Investing in the hardware and other infrastructure required to give each classroom Internet connectivity is an outcome of the school's commitment to supporting student project activity. The same principal has led also to outfitting the library with eight IBM clones that use sophisticated software to facilitate information and reference searches.

To support its vision of a self-motivated, self-directed student population, the school invests in a fairly high level of staff development. In Taylorsville's educational paradigm, teachers serve as facilitators for student learning. Teacher fluency and comfort in using information technology determines the success of the model. In the first two years of implementation, staff received six full days of technology training per year. Thereafter, two days a year have been devoted specifically to ongoing training in technology. A full-time technology coordinator assists teachers with their technology-related problem solving. The full-time technology coordinator has the assistance of three part-time aides.

Qualities Shared by Five Technology-Rich Schools

These five schools obviously have different objectives, serve different populations, and use technology in quite different ways. But they share common practices important for public policy development. We note the following:

- Each of the schools is "learner-centered," placing emphasis on the individual treatment of students according to their needs and capabilities. Perhaps the most explicit attention to this issue is found at the Taylorsville school where a computer-based instructional management system is used to support the development and use of individual student instructional strategies. Northbrook emphasizes clusters of students and teachers who stay together for several years so that they can know one another well. East Bakersfield has students develop individual portfolios that help them understand what they know and need to know to find productive roles after graduation.

- Each of the schools seemed to utilize and emphasize curriculum frameworks to ensure that the goals for student outcomes were clearly understood. The Christopher Columbus school program was put in place after an effort of several years to develop a curriculum framework and strategy by the Union City district. Taylorsville used standards developed by the Modern Red School House design team at the Hudson Institute to guide its educational offerings. Blackstock used the California frameworks that were in existence before the school reform started. In the view of the authors, the workshop was notable for the emphasis each of the school leaders placed on the learning that was to take place as opposed to focusing on the features of the technology that existed.

- Each of the schools had a density of computers that far exceeds that which is common in schools today. In fact, in all cases but one, the density exceeded the average density of the top 4 percent of schools, which is 3.9 students per computer (Table 2.2). The ubiquitous access to computers in most of these schools makes many of their programmatic features possible.

- All the schools had restructured their programs substantially. Class periods were lengthened and interdisciplinary programs introduced to retain necessary subject coverage. Project-based learning received considerable attention, but several of the schools also made use of more traditional drill and practice programs. Blackstock and Northbrook had substantially modified their buildings to facilitate and exploit the use of technology.

- Each of the school programs appeared to be the product of a fairly concentrated development effort. The character of the school had not simply evolved over time as more and more equipment arrived. Instead, explicit, focused development efforts were undertaken. Some were whole school developments, as was the case with Taylorsville, Northbrook, and Christopher Columbus. Alternatively, some had initially focused on one facet of a larger vision, as appears to have been the case in Blackstock and East Bakersfield.

- Each school's development was pushed forward by an initial increment of external funding. The sources were varied. The California schools received funds from a state technology program. The Christopher Columbus school had Chapter I and private sector funds. The Taylorsville school received funding from New American Schools Development Corporation. Northbrook got initial startup funds from its district and has sustained its development with additional grants and Chapter I funds. Thus the creation of a radically changed school (whether or not it is technology rich) requires an initial investment that defrays the exceptional costs of startup—both training and the technology itself.

- Relations among adults in the schools appeared changed. While this issue was not addressed by all the school leaders, several noted that there was considerably more consultation among teachers about the curriculum and about the progress of individual students. At Blackstock, the lead teachers in the smart classrooms appear to have adopted roles of assisting other staff with issues related to technology, curriculum, and instruction.

- School outcomes were described in rich ways. While it appears that all the schools showed some or major improvement against traditional accountability measures, many other indicators were used. Increased student and parent engagement, better job placement success, strong support from students and parents, and improved attendance were all cited.

- And not least, the annual per-student technology and technology-related cost for these pioneer technology-rich schools ranges between under three and over five times the average $70–$80 per student for all U.S. schools.

These schools are probably representative of the best practices across the nation. The whole school has been involved, not just one or two teachers. The instructional program has been changed to exploit technology. As hinted in Table 2.5, each of these schools is reported to have improved the learning of substantial portions of its students. Whether these schools are representative of high tech schools of the future is an open question, however. Technology is changing rapidly, and educators are still in the comparatively early stages of exploring ways in which learning can be enhanced by the application of technology.

Table 2.5

High-Technology Schools

School	Population	Computers/Students	Notable Features	Cited Outcomes
Blackstock Jr High School, Port Hueneme, CA	65% Hispanic, 76% Chapter I	1:2	"Smart" classrooms designed by faculty given year leave; emphasis on facility design; Incremental implementation over 8 years	Improved test scores; increased student learning abilities, comprehension, motivation, attitude; strong student, parent and teacher support
Christopher Columbus Middle School, Union City, NJ	91% Hispanic, 79% free lunch program	1:3	Emphasis on 111- and 148-minute time blocks and whole-language philosophy, computers in homes	Rising test scores on state tests, improved student attendance, reduced Chapter I requirements
East Bakersfield High School, Bakersfield, CA	60% Hispanic, very LEP[a] population	1:8	Emphasis on preparation for work; CAD/CAM,[b] business Systems; disk portfolios retained by students	Improved student retention; improved job placement
Northbrook Middle School, Houston, TX	Large Hispanic population, low SES[c]	1:2	Newly renovated school; 90-minute time blocks; individualized instruction; computer-assisted instruction	Test scores up sharply (attributed to whole school design)
Taylorsville Elem School, Taylorsville, IN	Suburban with largely white middle-class population	1:4	Major emphasis on instructional management system incorporating standards, curriculum, student plans and student work	Increased student interest and enthusiasm for learning; some improvement in test scores; program only two years old.

[a]Limited English proficiency.
[b]Computer-assisted design/computer-assisted manufacturing.
[c]Socioeconomic status.

THE EFFECTIVENESS OF EDUCATIONAL TECHNOLOGY

These technology-rich schools use technology in many different ways, which suggest the difficulty one has in making broad, inclusive, research-based statements concerning the effectiveness of educational technology. In them, technology is used, among other things, to tutor students, to support collaboration among students and teachers, to acquire educational resources from remote locations, to aid teachers in the assessment of student progress and the management of instruction, and to help students to write and compute. In some cases, technology is just one of a number of strategies for achieving an educational purpose—for example, teaching and learning introductory algebra. In others, it may be the only way to achieve some goal—distance learning to provide foreign language instruction to small, remote schools.

In trying to assess what is known concerning the effectiveness of technology, we held a workshop that engaged both researchers who have studied the effectiveness of technology applications in education and practitioners who have been associated with the development of schools making heavy use of technology. We discussed what is known about the effects, costs, and implementation in technology-intensive schools and programs. We also examined several recent reviews of the literature on the effectiveness of various technology applications. On the basis of the workshop and the reviews, we draw the following broad conclusions:

- Numerous studies of a wide variety of specific applications of technology show improvements in student performance, student motivation, teacher satisfaction, and other important educational outcomes.

- There are examples of technology-rich schools that report significant improvements in student motivation, academic outcomes, and other outcomes such as problem-solving or collaboration.

- Traditional ways of assessing the effectiveness of educational programs are generally deficient for assessing the contribution of technology.

- Good implementation is crucial to the successful application of technology in education.

We treat each of these points briefly.

Evidence on the Effectiveness of Educational Programs Making Extensive Use of Technology

The history of computers in education can be traced to sometime in the mid-1960s, with its start under the name "computer-assisted instruction" (CAI). The initial efforts to develop and deploy CAI reflected the mid-60s improvements in computer technology, emerging scientific hypotheses about learning largely based on the ideas associated with B. F. Skinner, and federally funded research and development (R&D) and operating subsidies aimed at improving the achievement of slow learners.

By now, CAI applications have been ported across several generations of computer technology, including large time-shared systems, smaller minicomputer systems, and the currently popular file-server technology. Interactive drill-and-practice software is a major school application of computers today, and the dominant application in elementary school education. This interactive modality is also widely used in military training and adult education. Because of the long history of these applications, there is a large body of evaluative data on the effectiveness of these applications.

One participant in the workshop, James Kulik, has spent more than a decade analyzing studies of the use of computers for instruction. He has summarized that work in a recent article[15] which begins,

> What do evaluation studies say about computer-based instruction? It is not easy to give a simple answer to the question. The term *computer-based instruction* has been applied to too many different programs, and the term *evaluation* has been used in too many different ways.

He goes on to describe a research approach, called meta-analysis, which has allowed him and others to aggregate research findings of many studies of computer-based instruction. He summarizes these findings as follows:

---

[15]Kulik, 1994.

At least a dozen meta-analyses involving over 500 individual studies have been carried out to answer questions about the effectiveness of computer-based instruction. The analyses were conducted independently by research teams at eight different research centers. The research teams focused on different uses of the computer with different populations, and they also differed in the methods they used to find studies and analyze study results. Nonetheless, each of the analyses yielded the conclusion that programs of computer-based instruction have a positive record in the evaluation literature.[16]

Kulik draws the following conclusions from his work.

1. Students usually learn more in classes in which they receive computer-based instruction. . . .

2. Students learn their lessons in less time with computer-based instruction. . . .

3. Students also like their classes more when they receive computer help in them. . . .

4. Students develop more positive attitudes toward computers when they receive help from them in school. . . .

5. Computers do not, however, have positive effects in every area in which they were studied. The average effect of computer-based instruction in 34 studies of attitude toward subject matter was near zero. . . .

Reporting approximately the same range of effect sizes from studies of military training as Kulik does for education, J. D. Fletcher[17] emphasizes the importance (measured by cost-effectiveness) for military training of performance outcomes (as opposed to knowledge acquisition outcomes[18]) and the training *time* necessary to reach a required level of task performance. In brief, studies of computer-

---

[16]Kulik, 1994, p. 11.

[17]A more extensive discussion of Fletcher's data can be found in Melmed, 1995.

[18]While performance outcomes for any nontrivial task are no doubt linked to knowledge acquisition, a current criticism of K–12 education is that knowledge acquisition often seems only weakly linked to performance in the "real" world.

based instruction in military training repeatedly show gains of about one-third in training time.

Fletcher introduced an additional set of calculations, based on meta analyses, that shed light on the potential "cost-effectiveness" of using computer-based instruction. He compared the costs of additional tutoring, reduced class size, increased instruction time or computer-based instruction required to obtain comparable gains in outcomes. Computer-based instruction was substantially less expensive than all other approaches to obtaining these gains except tutoring by peers.[19]

The computer-based instructional programs that provide the base for the studies reviewed by Kulik and Fletcher were largely developed and implemented before 1990. They tended to emphasize drill and practice. In recent years, the continued decline in the costs of computing power, the growth of both local area and wide area networking, and the development of increasingly sophisticated computer software has led to the rapid proliferation of applications that move beyond drill and practice.

This proliferation reflects at least two major influences. The first is the explosive growth in importance of information technology in the workplace and the perception that the skills required to succeed in future workplaces will be quite different from those that motivated the development of much of the curriculum that currently dominates schools.[20] The second is a growing body of research in the cognitive sciences that suggests that students learn and better retain what they learn when engaged in "authentic" learning tasks.[21] In school practice, this often takes the form of an individual or a small group of students carrying out real world projects using computer and network software tools and databases. In addition to improved subject matter learning, students develop their skills in cooperation, communication, and problem identification with this approach.

For these applications of technology, the research data are less extensive and not as well organized. The applications of technology are so varied and fluid that they defy attempts at aggregation. Moreover,

---

[19]Fletcher, Hawley, and Piele, 1990, pp. 783–806, as quoted in Melmed, 1995.

[20]See, for example, Secretary's Commission on Achieving Necessary Skills, 1991.

[21]See, for example, Resnick, 1987a, pp. 13–20; Resnick, 1987b; and Raizen, 1989.

the evaluation techniques that are appropriate to these newer uses are less standardized. Still, an accumulation of many individual studies show positive effects of specific programs on student and/or teacher attitudes and performance.[22]

At least one R&D program has focused directly on the effects of providing ubiquitous access to technology at the classroom level. Apple Classrooms of Tomorrow (ACOT) focused on the changed instructional practices and the learning by children when teachers and students are provided "access to technology whenever they need it."[23] For example, in its initial years, before the advent of laptops, each student and teacher was given two computers, one for home and one for school.

In a report on 10 years of ACOT research, the ACOT project says:

> Over time, independent researchers found that students in ACOT classrooms not only continued to perform well on standardized tests but were also developing a variety of competencies not usually measured. ACOT students did the following

- Explored and represented information dynamically and in many forms.

- Became socially aware and more confident.

- Communicated effectively about complex processes.

- Used technology routinely and appropriately.

- Became independent learners and self-starters.

- Knew their areas of expertise and shared that expertise spontaneously.

- Worked well collaboratively.

- Developed a positive orientation to the future.[24]

---

[22]See, for example, Means and Olson, 1995; Software Publishers Association, 1995; and Special Issue on Educational Technologies: Current Trends and Future Directions, 1994.

[23]Apple Computer Inc., 1995, p. 2.

[24]Apple Computer Inc., 1995, p. 3.

Thus, at the program, project, and classroom level, there is solid evidence that instructional activities making intensive use of technology can lead to significant improvements in student achievements. As is the case with any educational program, the success in replications of a technology-based application depends upon the quality of the implementation.

Individual programs are different from whole schools, however, and whole schools constitute a major focus for this report. What sort of evidence do we have concerning the effectiveness of technology-rich schools?

Evidence Concerning the Performance of Technology-Rich Schools

Policymakers, considering significant investments in technology for schools to improve learning generally, would like assurances that such investments will in fact provide this improved learning. It is difficult to provide such assurances if one wants to use traditional evaluation designs.

For example, to try to obtain such evidence, we could imagine conducting an experiment. From a large group of schools that are interested in implementing a technology-rich program, a randomly selected subgroup of schools is provided with resources to be used to purchase and use new technology throughout the school. Another subgroup of schools is chosen to serve as a control group. If, at the end of some period of time during which their programmatic changes were implemented, the technology-rich schools, as a group, were performing significantly better, we would be justified in saying that the use of technology had a positive effect on schooling outcomes.

The evidence we can cite is far less persuasive than would be the results of this imaginary experiment. Schools that have become technology rich have not been randomly chosen. Instead they have been led by individuals or groups who usually had a gift for attracting funds to support technology and for promoting widespread use of the technology in their schools. These schools' performance is not normally compared with other control schools but with their own earlier performance or with district averages on outcome variables.

Despite the uniqueness of these schools, it is useful to examine their experiences for suggestive evidence concerning the effects and effectiveness of technology.

One source of such experience is the five technology-rich schools represented at our workshop. From these, we had reports of improved student attitude and engagement, resulting from livelier classroom content; improved student achievement, measured by norm-standardized tests; improved student retention and improved job placement of secondary school graduates; and increased student enthusiasm for learning, together with an increased student commitment to the responsibility for learning.

To achieve these results, the leadership and teaching staffs of these pioneer schools took an individual, eclectic approach, sometimes emphasizing student computer projects in the context of a well-defined curriculum framework; sometimes combining subject matter like mathematics and science education or English and social studies in a single 90- or 140-minute class that allowed increased time for computer use; sometimes employing computer-based instruction, especially for teaching basic skills; and sometimes assigning word processing or desktop publishing tasks aimed at preparing students for the world of work. What stood out, in fact, was the variety and nonuniformity of the approaches technology-rich schools followed in their effort to improve student learning. Implementation strategies were ad hoc and local.

Another group of technology-rich schools was examined in a study sponsored by the U.S. Department of Education in an effort to understand how technology contributed to education reform.[25] Means and Olson examined eight schools, five of which would be termed technology rich because they had student-computer ratios of less than 2 to 1.[26] While Means and Olson's research did not emphasize student outcomes, the schools were asked about these outcomes. Most schools chose not to emphasize standard test scores and talked of improved student motivation, collaboration, and acquisition of skills not measured by normal tests. On balance, test scores on tra-

---

[25]Means and Olson, 1995.

[26]Of the other three, one had 12 students per computer and the other two had ratios of 7 and 8 to 1, respectively.

ditional tests were up somewhat, but there were a few cases in which they dipped. It is important to note that from the description of the programs provided by Means and Olson, it appears that traditional examinations are poorly aligned with the curriculum and pedagogy of most of these schools.[27]

Rather than student outcomes, the Means and Olson study focused on the manner in which technology fosters educational reform, specifically, constructivist teaching.[28] In this regard, their conclusions are less equivocal. With regard to instructional practice they found that technology supported improved instruction by

- adding to students' perceptions that their work is authentic and important

- increasing the complexity with which students can deal successfully

- dramatically enhancing student motivation and self-esteem

- making obvious the need for long blocks of [instructional] time

- instigating greater collaboration, with students helping peers and sometimes their teachers

- giving teachers additional impetus to take on a coaching and advisory role.

---

[27]Means and Olson, 1995, pp. 38–53 and Table 9. It is worth noting that in the studies described in the previous subsection dealing with well-specified programs, many of the assessments used were chosen because they *were* aligned with the curriculum. However, the tests the whole school reforms are judged on are the ones specified by the state or district for accountability purposes.

[28]Means and Olson, 1995, pp. 2–3. Drawing on the work of cognitive scientists, the authors state

> This constructivists' view of learning, with its call for teaching basic skills within authentic contexts (hence more complex problems), for modeling expert thought processes, and for providing for collaboration and external supports to permit students to achieve intellectual accomplishments that they could not do on their own, provides the conceptual underpinnings for our investigation of technology's role in education reform.

Teachers also talked of increases in their skills in technology and pedagogy and increased collaboration.[29]

While these few examples of schools providing technology-rich learning environments are, in our view, encouraging, they are scant. In framing their policy conclusions, Means and Olson note:

> We believe that the difficulty we experienced in finding schools with large numbers of classrooms incorporating technology-supported constructivist teaching and learning approaches is in itself a significant finding. The scarcity of these classrooms testifies to the magnitude of the change we are looking for and the challenges— individual, organizational, and logistical—to making it happen.[30]

Means and Olson selected their schools in 1993. Our experience in seeking sites to participate in our workshop in early 1995, while less extensive than that of Means and Olson, suggests that such schools remain comparatively rare. Thus, research has not yet identified a sufficient number of examples of technology-supported whole school reforms to allow us to fully gauge the contributions that educational technology can be reliably expected to make to reform objectives. One recommendation we will make is that the nation seek out the early-adopting pioneer schools for continued study and assessment to improve our knowledge of the impacts of technology-rich learning environments on students and teachers.

A Note of Caution from History

We have repeatedly used the phrase "properly implemented" in our discussions of the effectiveness of technology-supported instruction. This is an important caveat. While computer- and network-based technology is currently the focus of most public attention, the nation has a long history of trying to reform education through the use of technologies such as radio, motion pictures, and television. On the whole, these attempted reforms were unsuccessful although isolated instances of effective use exist.

---

[29]Means and Olson, 1995, pp. S-2 and S-3.

[30]Means and Olson, 1995, p. S-5.

Larry Cuban has examined the history of attempts to use technology to promote reform of schools.[31] He concludes that most of these attempts failed to adequately address the real needs of teachers in classrooms. Instead, the efforts too often attempted to impose a technologist's or policymaker's vision of the appropriate use of the technology on schools. Teachers were provided inadequate assistance in using the technology, and the technology itself was often unreliable. As a consequence, the technology was not used by teachers or became very marginal to the schools' instructional activities.

These lessons are important and have been recognized in the schools we examined. The pioneer schools have involved teachers deeply in the development of their programs. The ACOT program makes teachers and their needs its central focus. If technology-rich learning environments are to be created in many schools, policymakers and educators will need to attend to these lessons and avoid standardized implementation of prepackaged technical solutions.

Conclusion

As we have seen, there are two important impediments to obtaining defensible, research-based information on the performance of most applications of technology in schools. First, most available tests do not reliably measure the outcomes that are being sought by advocates of technology-rich schools. The measures that are reported are usually from traditional, multiple choice tests. Second, technology is only a component of an instructional activity. Assessments of the impact of technology are really assessments of instructional processes enabled by technology, and the outcomes are highly dependent on the quality of the implementation of the entire instructional process.

The review that we made of evidence of the effectiveness of educational technology reaffirmed our initial impressions. By traditional evaluation standards, the most satisfying evaluation data are those generated in laboratory or controlled clinical settings using well-specified and implemented treatments and readily measured outcomes. When technology is removed from such settings and be-

---

[31]Cuban, 1995; see also Tyack and Cuban, 1995.

comes more nearly a tool to be used by students and teachers than a treatment in itself, or when the outcomes sought become richer and less precisely measurable, assessment becomes much more difficult and the results less satisfying from a technical point of view.

Despite these difficulties, however, evidence and experience suggest that there are a number of technology-rich schools with effectively implemented instructional programs that provide exciting and apparently successful demonstrations of the potential that educational technology has for improving the quality of schooling and learning. The question that we now want to turn to is what are the technology-related costs of implementing technology-rich programs such as those described here.

Chapter Three

THE COSTS OF TECHNOLOGY-RICH SCHOOLS

Chapter Two provided descriptions both of what is and what could be. The shape of the future use of technology to facilitate learning depends upon the decisions that are made by schools, school systems, states, teachers, and families. In turn, their decisions will largely be based on their perceptions concerning the importance and value of that technology. In this chapter, we want to explore the costs of acquiring learning environments that utilize significant levels of computing, telecommunications, and video.

We begin with a brief effort to estimate current expenditures for education and then go on to look at the costs of the technology that was used by the group of schools that were described in Chapter Two. We use those data to make rough estimates of the continuing costs associated with decisions to equip schools and school faculties with equipment and capabilities similar to those in the schools we examined. Naturally, this implies a significant increase in technology-related expenditures over what is currently spent.

Much of the current impetus to bring more technology into schools is not motivated by a desire to improve the learning of students in academic areas. Instead it is motivated by the sense that information and computational technology has become so ubiquitous in our lives that schools must develop the basic skills in students so that they can function in further schooling and work. Moving to the levels of technology in the five schools described in the preceding chapter accomplishes this goal but adds much more. Increasing the level of technology enables fundamental changes in pedagogy, in the information that students can use, and in the manner in which they use their time. These changes result in significant improvements in their learning.

CURRENT SCHOOL TECHNOLOGY EXPENDITURE

We can make a rough estimate of the current average per-student cost for school technology, including computer and communications hardware and software, and related expenditures for training and personnel. In 1994–95, the fall enrollment was 44.2 million. The current expenditure per enrolled pupil was about $5,600, and total current expenditures were about $249 billion.[1]

Estimates from QED and others suggest that public school systems purchased approximately a million new personal computers (PCs) in 1994–95. Pricing a computer at $1,500 on average, expenditures for hardware would be $1.5 billion. On the basis of information from the Software Publishers Association and attendees at RAND's software workshops, expenditures for software were on the order of $750 million. A major market survey estimated that expenditures for training were about half those for software.[2] These costs then total about $2.6 billion. Costs of networking, additional personnel, and other costs might add another $400 to $600 million to provide a crude estimate of $3 to $3.2 billion.

If these costs are roughly correct, they imply a per-student expenditure for technology of about $70, or somewhat less than 1.3 percent of current public expenditures for elementary and secondary education, or 1.1 percent of total expenditures including capital.[3]

---

[1]These figures are taken from National Center for Education Statistics (NCES), 1995c, Table 34; and NCES, 1995b. They are estimates for the school year ending in 1995. Total expenditures (including capital) were actually $280 billion or about $6,336 per enrolled student.

[2]This is based on a 1993 survey by Market Data Retrieval, Inc., that is reported in OTA, 1995, p. 136.

[3]In a recent report based on interviews with a sample of technology coordinators in school districts, QED estimated that the expenditures were about $3.6 billion for school year 1994–95. See *New York Times,* 1995. One problem with comparing national estimates of costs is that the definitions that are used are not necessarily consistent. Some probably include administrative as well as instructional applications. (The distinction between the two is not always clear.) Expenditures for teacher training may be understated as well since some of these are incurred by the teachers them-

COSTS OF INCREASING THE LEVEL OF TECHNOLOGY IN SCHOOLS

Technology has and will continue to change rapidly. Those changes have lowered costs for a given level of capability but have often spurred the development of software that requires greater capabilities. Wireless networking technology promises to reduce the costs of networks where building renovations are substantial or where a site is geographically isolated. The power requirements of many new computers have been reduced. Moreover, the manner in which such technology will be introduced and used will vary greatly from school to school and district to district. Thus future costs of educational technology are necessarily uncertain.

As a consequence, for this study, we have sought to develop only a broad estimate of the order of magnitude of the costs of introducing technology into a school. In essence, we have examined the costs of the equipment and associated training in a small number of schools that were nominated by experts as examples of schools that were effectively using technology. We have used these costs, together with estimates of student populations, to provide the reader a sense of the magnitude of costs for more intensive use of technology.[4]

The data collection that we undertook is described in another RAND report.[5] The approach was straightforward. We asked experts to

---

selves and some are components of other staff development efforts. Therefore, it is best to treat these as rough estimates of magnitude.

[4]Several efforts are under way to develop a clearer understanding of the costs of introducing technology into schools. The most extensive appears to be that by McKinsey & Company done for the National Information Infrastructure Advisory Committee. As this was being written, the report had not been formally submitted. The McKinsey effort envisions several models of school use of technology and costs the introduction of such technology into schools over 5 and 10 year periods, as well as costing operating and maintaining the equipment once it is in place. While the report is currently confidential, the drafts we have examined suggest national cost estimates that are similar to those that we discuss in this section.

[5]Keltner and Ross, 1996. Note that three additional schools were surveyed by Keltner and Ross. The Corona school in Los Angeles is a technology magnet funded, in part, with a California State Technology Grant. Elizabeth Street School is a K–12 school in Los Angeles that is a part of the New American Schools Development Corporation. The ALL School in Worcester, Massachusetts, is also a NASDC school, and the design is under the direction of Bolt, Beranek, and Newman. These three schools were not

suggest schools that they thought made effective use of technology. The schools were chosen to be representative of a spectrum of student populations and grade levels. Many of them were described in the previous chapter.

Table 3.1 shows the major technology cost components for the schools we examined. The cost figures shown are normally not the actual historical costs but rather a cost estimate based on the *amortized* cost of the current installation, valued at today's prices. More specifically, the following rules and assumptions were used:

- The current equipment inventory was used.

- Current prices were used for all computer hardware.

- The cost of hardware and software products was amortized over five years.

- The cost of infrastructure, such as special furniture and cabling, was amortized over ten years.

- The cost of any initial teacher preparation was amortized over five years.

- The cost of new personnel and materials and supplies was treated as an annual expense.

Our aim was to examine factors affecting total cost; to relate cost with purpose, when possible; to consider how cost might affect financing; and to use these data to prepare some projections for the cost of a nation of technology-enabled schools.

These *annualized* cost figures do not provide a good picture of the level of front-end investment required to implement a technology strategy. We believe that technology costs should come to be viewed by schools as a recurring expense, because technology is central to a school's operations. Our treatment of costs in annualized terms is consistent with this vision. However, if we assume that schools start with virtually no equipment and phase the equipment and training in over a three-year period, the costs might be approximately 70 per-

explicitly included in our workshop because they did not yet seem to have had enough experience.

cent greater in each of those first three years. Putting this more concretely, for schools near the high end of costs in Table 3.1 with annualized costs of $450 per student, the front end costs for a 1,000-student school might be $2.3 million spread over three years. This would include the training of teachers and administrators.

Not all these costs need be met by additional funds. For example, training costs might be supported by existing funds for staff development or by the staffs' own investments in their professional development. There are also resources for additional staff built into these costs; these might be met by redefining the functions of some of the existing staff members. Finally, some schools will already possess some of the equipment and/or infrastructure. Thus the costs of implementing the designs represented by the various schools we examined will differ in alternative settings.

Factors Affecting School-Level Costs

The data presented in Table 3.1 cannot be considered representative in any statistical sense. Nonetheless, they provide some interesting insights into distribution of costs in schools that have made heavy investments in technology and that have integrated the technology into their education programs. The following is particularly noteworthy:

1. The range of costs per student is wide; from around $180 to $450 per student (ignoring the lowest and highest outlying cost figures). Assuming a national average current expenditure of $5,600 per student, this range represents about 3 to 7 percent of the current expenditures for educating a student, compared with our estimate of existing expenditures of 1.3 percent of current expenditures.

2. The primary factor affecting total annualized student cost is equipment, especially computer hardware density, i.e., the student-to-computer ratio. Except at the low end of per-pupil cost, where certain fixed costs play an important role, total cost is decisively affected by this factor. Table 3.2 and Figure 3.1 summarize the relationship of annualized per-student cost to student-to-computer ratio in this sample of eight schools.

Table 3.1

Comparative Cost Figures for Eight Schools

	Corona	E. Bakersfield	Elizabeth St.	Taylorsville	Blackstock	ALL School	Northbrook	CC
Total annual cost	$169,863	$299,835	$331,542	$227,942	$381,340	$233,018	$348,450	$151,940
Annual cost per student	$142	$182	$184	$371	$410	$432	$453	$490
Student total	1,200	1650	1,800	615	930	540	770	310
Ratio, Student: computer units	11:1	8:1	9:1	4:1	2:1	4:1	2:1	3:1
Hardware subtotal	$50,343	$133,400	$140,341	$110,619	$213,650	$100,258	$232,600	$57,790
Software subtotal	$16,600	$11,620	$24,700	$23,633	$38,760	$15,300	$14,200	$15,800
Infrastructure	$8,040	$14,905	$19,001	$5,000	$22,930	$6,900	$24,750	$8,300
Staff Dev.	$24,880	$24,840	$26,500	$15,690	$85,000	$13,760	$19,400	$11,050
Personnel	$62,000	$105,000	$100,000	$69,000	$12,500	$92,000	$42,500	$50,000
Materials	$8,000	$10,000	$21,000	$4,000	$8,500	$4,800	$15,000	$9,000

Table 3.1—continued

	Corona	E. Bakersfield	Elizabeth St.	Taylorsville	Blackstock	ALL School	Northbrook	CC
				Percentages				
Hardware subtotal	29.64	44.51	42.33	48.53	56.03	43.03	66.75	38.03
Software subtotal	9.77	3.88	7.45	10.37	10.16	6.57	4.08	10.40
Infrastructure	4.73	4.97	5.73	2.19	6.01	2.96	7.10	5.46
Staff Dev.	14.65	8.28	7.99	6.88	22.29	5.91	5.57	7.27
Personnel	36.50	35.02	30.16	30.27	3.28	39.48	12.20	32.91
Materials	4.71	3.34	6.33	1.75	2.23	2.06	4.30	5.92
				Per Student				
Hardware subtotal	$41.95	$80.89	$77.97	$179.87	$229.73	$185.66	$302.08	$186.42
Software subtotal	$13.83	$7.04	$13.72	$38.43	$41.68	$28.33	$18.44	$50.97
Infrastructure	$6.70	$9.03	$10.56	$8.13	$24.66	$12.78	$32.14	$26.77
Staff Dev.	$20.73	$15.05	$14.72	$25.51	$91.40	$25.48	$25.19	$35.65
Personnel	$51.67	$63.64	$55.56	$112.20	$13.44	$170.37	$55.19	$161.29
Materials	$6.67	$6.06	$11.67	$6.50	$9.14	$8.89	$19.48	$29.03

NOTE: Costs annualized according to rules explained on page 50.

Table 3.2

Technology-Related Costs in Selected Schools
(annualized costs per student)

School	Cost Per Student	Students Per Computer
Corona (Los Angeles, CA)	$142	11:1
E. Bakersfield, (Bakersfield, CA)	$182	8:1
Elizabeth St. (Los Angeles, CA)	$184	9:1
Taylorsville (Taylorsville, IN)	$371	4:1
Blackstock (Port Hueneme, CA)	$410	2:1
ALL School (Worcester, MA)	$432	4:1
Northbrook (Houston, TX)	$453	2:1
Christopher Columbus (Union City, NJ)	$490	3:1

SOURCE: Keltner and Ross, 1996.

3. Other computer hardware products associated with intra-school networks (LANs) add to the total hardware cost; for schools favoring them, such as E. Bakersfield, Elizabeth St., and the ALL School, audio/video equipment could add substantially to total annualized cost.

4. A second major factor affecting total cost is personnel. All of these schools found it necessary to have continuing staff who were clearly devoted to supporting technology operations. In some cases, individuals were newly hired to provide specific technical services associated with the technology implementation. In others, teachers became a combination of technical expert and a source of assistance to other teachers who were seeking better ways to integrate technology with their program.[6]

5. Staff development ranged from $15 to $35 per student with most schools spending on the order of $25. One exceptional school, Blackstock, spent over $90 per student, but this represented the

---

[6]As noted in the text, the salaries of these personnel did not necessarily constitute an incremental cost to the school. In some cases, existing personnel were assigned new duties and in at least one case, teachers agreed to a slightly higher class load so that the school could hire a technology specialist to help them.

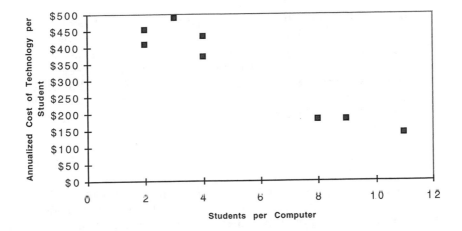

Figure 3.1—Relation of Annualized Cost Per Student to Computer Density

unusual way in which the school chose to introduce technology. At Blackstock, a number of lead teachers were provided a year off from their classroom duties to develop new programs utilizing technology so that the term "staff development" really understates the nature of the teacher's experience in this case.[7]

6. The per-student cost of software is low, between 4 and 10 percent of the total, and much lower than the cost of software for typical enterprise computing, where it can reach parity with hardware cost.

When the costs are tallied in the manner they are in Tables 3.1 and 3.2, they are significant. If all schools in the United States were to spend an increment of $450 per student, near the top of the estimated annualized costs of the schools we examined, the total would be about $20 billion, or 8 percent of the estimated total current ex-

---

[7]It is important to note that Keltner and Ross assumed that teachers involved with staff development would be compensated for their time—either through time when relieved from classroom duties (with a substitute being hired) or through a stipend for additional time. This assumption is made no matter what arrangements were made by the actual school and was done to increase comparability of the estimates.

penditure per student.[8] If, instead, we adopt a cost per student more nearly in line with the lower end of our sample of schools—perhaps $180 per student (see Figure 3.1)—the annualized cost is $8 billion, or 3.2 percent of current expenditures. As we noted in the last section, these expenditures compare with an estimated $3.1 billion, or 1.2 percent of current expenditures that was devoted to technology in the 1994–95 school year. These calculations are summarized in Table 3.3.

These are national averages. State-level data show that in 1991-92, when average current per-pupil expenditures were $5,594, the state level averages ranged from a low of $3,180 (Utah) to a high of $9,415 (New Jersey).[9] Within-state variations are also quite wide so that, as measured by current per-pupil expenditures, states and districts vary substantially in the resources that they can draw upon. Since most of the prices for equipment and software are set in national markets, we might expect that the density of computers would be correlated to this expenditure level.

However, decisions to fund educational technology are not necessarily well correlated with an indicator of "ability to pay," such as

Table 3.3

Annualized Expenditures for Educational Technology in Public K–12 Schools for Several Levels of Investment

	Technology Expenditures Per Student	Annual Expenditures for Education Technology (billions of dollars)	Percentage of Current K–12 Expenditures
Current	$70	3.1	1.2
Moderate	$180	8.0	3.2
High	$450	19.9	8.0

NOTE: For public K–12 schools with 1994–95 fall enrollment of 44.2 million students and total expenditures of $6,300 per student.

---

[8]Four hundred fifty dollars per student times 44.2 million students in 1994–95. Current expenditures per student in 1994–95 are estimated at $5,623 while total expenditures per student are estimated at $6,336. Expenditure data are from NCES, 1995b, Table 163. Enrollment data are from the NCES, 1995c, Table 2, Chapter 2.

[9]NCES, 1995b, Table 164.

overall educational expenditures are. Figure 3.2 shows the situation for the three states with the highest overall ratios of students to computers and the three with the lowest ratios. While the number of computers per student differs by about a factor of two between these two groups of states, the expenditures per student on education are more nearly the same. Clearly, decisions that technology is important to education can lead states (and their constituent districts) to allocate increased proportions of their resources to technology.[10]

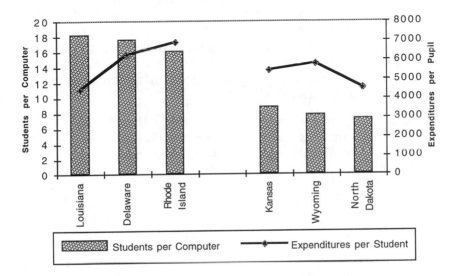

SOURCES: Computer density from QED, 1994; expenditures from NCES, 1995b.

Figure 3.2—Expenditures Per Student for States with Lowest and Highest Computer Densities

---

[10]The fact that the three states with low ratios of students to computers are substantially rural is almost certainly an important determinant here. It is quite likely that distance learning plays a more important role in these three states than in the other three. Remember also that in the previous chapter we cited evidence that computer densities tend to be higher in small schools, which are probably more prevalent in rural states.

Conclusion

The costs of providing technology-rich learning environments in the nation's schools are not inconsequential. Based on the experience of the schools we have examined, the costs range from $10 to $20 billion, depending on the richness of the environment assumed. These costs range from three to six times what is currently being spent for technology. However, when viewed in the context of the total public elementary and secondary school enterprise, the costs seem more modest, ranging from 3.2 to 8 percent of the current expenditures for the 1994–95 school year. Nonetheless, financing such costs will require either a willingness of the nation's taxpayers to increase the levels of spending for elementary and secondary education or for its school systems to undertake a significant and difficult reallocation of the resources they currently spend.

In the next chapter, we discuss this financing problem and then deal with two other challenges that face the nation as it deepens the level of technology in schools—the professional development of teachers and the shortage of content software.

Chapter Four

CHALLENGES OF CREATING A NATION OF TECHNOLOGY-ENABLED SCHOOLS

The previous chapters have provided a picture of the potential of learner-centered schools for making extensive use of technology for improving the performance of the education system in the United States. However, there are many challenges to realizing that potential. In this section, we want to deal with the three most important:

1. Financing the costs of creating and sustaining technology-rich schools.

2. Providing teachers with the skills and time needed to implement such schools.

3. Features of the educational software market that may restrict the supply of some important classes of software.

At the end of each subsection, we suggest possible actions that the public and private sectors can take to deal with these challenges.

FINANCING THE COSTS OF INTRODUCING AND USING TECHNOLOGY IN SCHOOLS

If policymakers want to significantly increase the level of technology in the schools, they face two key financial problems.

1. How does a school system obtain the resources for the initial investment necessary to transform a school into a technology-rich enterprise?

2. How does a school system obtain 3 to 5 percent (or more) of their budget per year to devote to technology and training on a continuing basis?

Past experience suggests that initial investment funding will be provided by a wide variety of means specific to the individual financial and political conditions of states and school districts. We believe that the continuing costs associated with extensive use of technology in all schools can only be achieved with significant restructuring of school budgets.

Front-End Investment

The schools examined in the Keltner and Ross (1996) cost study are representative of the current approach to investment for technology-rich schools. These schools have financed themselves with a combination of special grants, donations from business, fund-raising by parents, categorical funding from federal or state programs, and, occasionally, a little restructuring of a school's budget. Training has been supported by normal staff development funding as well as substantial "sweat equity" of committed teachers. Funding was pieced together by exceptional leaders, administrators, teachers, and parents who had unusual capabilities to identify and tap external sources of funds. Thus these schools are exceptions rather than the norm.[1]

This form of "expedient" financing is symptomatic of a deeply in-grained problem of social service providers in general and educational agencies in particular. Compared with the private sector, they lack an investment mentality.[2] School districts do not regularly set aside a specified portion of their revenues for investing in activities to

---

[1] The funding obtained by these schools was largely devoted to initial investments. Several of the schools reported that they were beginning to face problems with the sustained maintenance and updating of their capital stock. Many of the funding sources supported the investments but not the costs of long-term continuing operations.

[2] School systems do plan for building and renovating schools, but these activities are normally tied to specific bond issues and are not closely related to school programs. Requirements for networks and adequate power for technology are often part of these projects.

improve school performance. The reasons for this are found in the political nature of resource allocation in public education.

The allocation of resources in public school districts is a highly political process. The governance of school systems forces a superintendent and his or her staff to satisfy a large number of claimants. Teachers, other staff, advocates for students with special needs, schools with politically powerful parents, employers seeking a steady supply of job entrants, and government leaders seeking schools to enhance economic development all put pressures on the leaders of a school district. Funding restrictions may be imposed by state or federal governments in support of one or another interest that has made its needs known at higher levels of government.

To cope with these demands, many superintendents and their staffs adopt coping rather than strategic behaviors. The resulting budget is a product of political compromise intended to minimize political pain. Existing allocations of resources are the starting point and only marginal changes are made. Firm, long-term commitments of the type required to install technology throughout a system are seldom made. Such commitments restrict future capabilities to allocate funds, while key district actors prefer to keep their options open.

This behavior is reinforced by the difficulty of assessing the relative values of alternative investments. The sort of investment planning possible in the private sector is hampered by the lack of clear measures of outcome and an understanding of the link between investment actions and outcomes.

An example may illustrate this. Consider two quite different investment options. The first is an "academy" at which the district's staff can be trained or provided opportunities to plan with the assistance of specialized staff. Funds are required to build or renovate space, acquire necessary materials, and hire and train a staff. The returns are presumably improved programs in individual schools. The second option is investment in the technology infrastructure of a set of schools coupled with the training necessary to exploit that infrastructure.

Both of these alternatives are forms of investment. Both can plausibly be expected to yield a long-term return on the investment. However, generally agreed-to causal links between investment actions and learning outcomes are lacking, and the latter are difficult to measure. Under similar circumstances, private organizations might be able to use expert judgment in evaluating the alternatives, but for schools, this is complicated by the open nature of school decision-making.

Most decisions like these have to be made in public forums where virtually all decisions must be politically defensible. Aggregating resources for a strategic purpose inevitably means that resources must be taken from other activities. If widely agreed-to relations between investment acts and outcomes are not available, those losing resources will complain loudly and, if politically powerful, will be likely to prevail. It is easy to see why there is a tendency to spread resources among claimants rather than to mass resources for a strategic purpose.[3]

As with any broad generalization, there are important exceptions to this observation. Some districts have had a significant history of investing in technology for their schools. To develop a better understanding of how they operated, we interviewed administrators in 14 districts that have invested heavily in technology.[4] Several points stand out.

Taken as a whole, these districts relied heavily on their own local funding sources. Nearly half had made technology a part of one or more local bond issues that supported building expansion and renovation as well.[5] Many of the systems had moderately restructured their central office expenditures to free up funding. Several had strong support from the local business community; for example,

---

[3]This certainly should not be taken to say that such investment behaviors are impossible. For example, during the 1980s both superintendents Richard Wallace in Pittsburgh and Donald Ingwerson in Jefferson County, Kentucky, succeeded in introducing investment-like behaviors with the strong support of the business leaders in their communities.

[4]The work reported here was carried out by Karl Sun. The districts were chosen using QED's list of large districts rank-ordered by the number of students per computer. These districts had ratios of students to computers ranging from 4.1:1 to 7.5:1. QED, 1994, Appendix H.

[5]It appears that the payback periods for these bond issues were structured so that the part that supported the technology was paid in five to seven years, in keeping with the expected lifetime of the equipment.

Jefferson County, Kentucky, reported that 60 percent of the costs of acquiring computers were covered by the business community. Where state programs were available, schools took advantage of those funds. Only a few of the districts we surveyed reported making significant use of federal Title I or Title II funding.[6]

As would be expected with efforts funded largely by local sources, the respondents reported that the investments in technology seemed to have strong public support. The public felt that widespread use of computers and other technology was important and that the educational system was doing an effective job of deploying technology in its schools. As with other school reforms, good strategies for engaging the public are important.

While the school districts that we surveyed provide some guidance concerning the manner in which investments in technology can be fostered and an investment mentality developed, it is important to note some important caveats concerning this sample of districts. Because of the source and nature of the data used to select them, the 14 districts are all large ones with substantial student populations. Most are in regions that are experiencing population and/or economic growth. The sample does not include either small, resource-poor districts or urban districts that have lost much of both their tax base and their middle-class families. For many schools that fall into these groups, it is probably unreasonable to expect that the districts and schools can finance substantial technology and reform efforts wholly on their own.

We believe that if schools are going to significantly restructure themselves and if technology is to be a major element of the restructuring, an investment mentality must be engendered in state and local districts. There are several possible ways to do this.

1. Districts could decide to set aside a portion of their total funding explicitly for investment and develop decision procedures governing the use of these funds.

---

[6]These were sections of the Elementary and Secondary Education Act that supported funding for schools with high proportions of students from disadvantaged backgrounds and school improvement. The act has been reauthorized as the Improving America's Schools Act, with a substantially different program structure.

2. Communities could establish and fund independent foundations intended to support the acquisition and deployment of technology.

3. Higher levels of government, more insulated from local politics, could establish special funds or programs that can be used to support technology investments.

Each of these approaches intended to create a pool of resources that can be allocated in a manner that differs from a school district's normal budget allocation process.

District Set-Aside Funds. We are not aware of any district that formally allocates funds to an investment "account." However, funds are often allocated to staff and/or curriculum development activities. There are likely to be technology line items in some districts. There are funds for purchasing textbooks that may be allocated centrally. Each of these activities has an investment purpose although they may be treated as a current expense.

Funding for these activities (and others having an investment purpose) could be aggregated and an explicit investment planning process instituted. While these investments should not be restricted to technology, for districts that have decided that technology and its implementation should be a major investment activity, technology could constitute a major theme. Funds raised from the sale of bonds might also be allocated through the same investment planning process.

Decisions on the level of funding for investment should be a major concern of the school board, presumably based on the recommendation of the superintendent. A significant effort to engage the public in this activity would be necessary with a major goal being to establish the legitimacy of this means of allocating funds.

Community-Based Funds. We noted above that in one of the districts we interviewed, Jefferson County, the business community had established a local foundation over a decade ago with the explicit goal of putting computers in schools.[7] While this is the most ambi-

---

[7]See the Jefferson County case study in Beryl Buck Institute for Education, 1994.

tious example of a community fund for technology we know of, there are many examples of less formal agreements between businesses or collections of businesses and schools.

Creating a community fund allows the allocation of investment resources to be separated somewhat from the normal budget allocation process of the school system. Moreover, the actions of the fund can be coordinated with related activities by the district such as the allocation of funds for the support of professional development. In communities where business and local foundations exist, this may be an attractive option for supporting initial investment in technology.

State and Federal Funding. Quite a number of states have provided funds for technology. Some have explicitly sought to create networks (e.g., Texas and North Carolina). Others have provided funds for equipping schools and training staff (e.g., Ohio and Florida). Several have provided funds for exemplary projects (e.g., California and Kentucky). As we noted, while most of the districts we surveyed relied largely on local funds, 8 of the 14 mentioned state funding (including lottery funding) as a source of some funding.

Only 3 of the 14 districts surveyed mentioned federal funds as a primary funding source, but as we noted above, the districts we interviewed were generally ones for which federal funding was not very important. In fact, nationwide, perhaps 30 percent of the funding for technology in elementary and secondary education in 1994 came from federal sources.[8] Much of this was supported by Chapter I, the component of the Elementary and Secondary Education Act that provides resources to districts with high proportions of educationally disadvantaged students.[9]

Both the states and the federal government have the advantage that they are somewhat distant from the politics that focuses on district-

---

[8]It is estimated that the federal government provided about $850 million of the funds invested in educational technology and related training in 1994. Of this, more than half came from Chapter I. Interview with Charles Blaschke, Education Turnkey Systems, August 15, 1995.

[9]The changes incorporated in its recent reauthorization to expand the number of "whole school" Chapter I (now Title I) programs should make it an even more effective source of funds supporting technology for schools serving high proportions of economically and educationally disadvantaged children.

level allocations. As a consequence, both have placed more emphasis on investment both in technology itself and in training. While all levels of government are under heavy political pressure to hold down overall spending, future initial investments in technology almost certainly will require additional funding from sources above the local district.

Whether the funds come from improved local allocations, community-level foundations, or state and federal sources, it is important that they be seen as initial investments. Planning surrounding their use should anticipate the need for continuing expenditures for operations, maintenance, and replacement.

Continuing Costs of Operating Technology-Rich Schools

The capability to devote a steady level of funding to maintaining and updating the stock of educational technology and the school staff seems to us to be a somewhat (although not wholly) separate issue from that of making initial investments. Continuing support for technology-rich learning environments requires a significant restructuring of school and district-level budgets to permit the reallocation of resources from existing to new uses. Such a reallocation seems unlikely unless schools are given substantial authority over their entire budget, and school personnel and parents feel the reallocation will improve the education of their students. Obviously, decisions by individual schools to reallocate will depend upon solid information concerning the benefits associated with integrating technology into their educational program, strong support from the community, and the availability of the assistance that schools need to make the transformation from current programs to new ones.

Historically, there has been little inclination to make significant shifts in resources. Figure 4.1 shows the overall distribution of current expenses for K–12 education in the nation as a whole. About two-thirds of the resources are allocated either to instruction or to school administration at the school-building level. Instructional services include funding for curriculum development and staff training and are therefore a potential source for some of the resources needed to support a school in transition to a technology-enabled program.

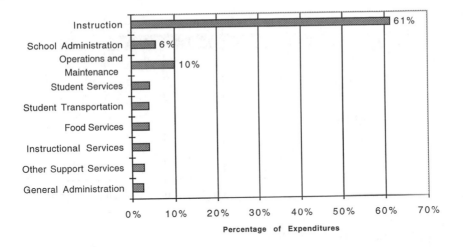

SOURCE: NCES, 1995b, Table 160.

Figure 4.1—Allocation of School Expenditures, 1992–93

The instructional budgets of the schools themselves are largely allocated to teaching staff. Figure 4.2 provides a further breakdown of the top bar (instruction) in Figure 4.1.

The most obvious source of funding for technology is the category "supplies," but, according to participants in our software workshop, at least half of those resources are devoted to textbooks and a quarter of the remainder goes to materials such as pencils, paper, and other supplies. Much of the rest does currently support instructional software. The purchased services and tuition-and-other categories may, in some instances, provide limited resources to support training and to purchase technical assistance.[10]

In short, the resource picture that is presented in Figures 4.1 and 4.2 suggests that the modest reallocations of existing budgets (possibly

---

[10]Our available study resources did not permit us to dig into any school budgets in detail. Our impression from discussions both at our workshops and with technology coordinators in schools is that the funds for technology at any particular site are likely to come from a wide variety of sources and that it would be quite impossible to track those costs back into the data underlying Figures 4.1 and 4.2. These charts simply provide a view of the relative magnitudes of classes of expenditures.

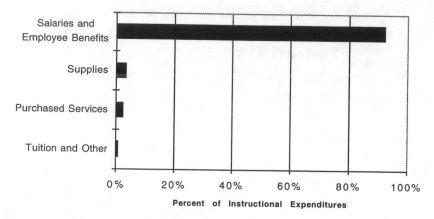

Percent of Instructional Expenditures

SOURCE: NCES, 1995b, Table 158.

**Figure 4.2—Distribution of Instructional Expenditures
Among Expenditure Categories, 1991–92**

supplemented with some additional capital funds from state or local bond issues) could be used to provide the $180 per student that we suggested in Table 3.3—always with the caveat that some schools and districts facing particularly difficult fiscal and student population challenges are exceptions to this generalization. Our assumed costs for technology in such schools was on the order of 3 percent of total educational costs (or 4.5 percent of expenditures at the school-building level).

The situation is different, however, for schools that are truly technology intensive. If we assume that such schools might have a continuing annualized cost of $450 per student for hardware, additional personnel, software and materials, and training, this cost constitutes nearly 8 percent of the expected national average, current, per-student expenditure of $5,600—or about 12 percent of the resources allocated directly to the school building. Clearly, this poses a different magnitude of difficulty.

There are existing sources of funding to offset some of these costs. The most obvious are the resources currently available in the form of released time for teachers, pupil free days, or other time for teacher planning and professional development. In some states and school systems, up to 10 or more days per teacher can be assembled if the school and its teachers act to effectively marshal these resources. Funding, either at the school level or in the central office can also provide resources for outside expertise necessary to support the effective implementation of a technology-rich learning environment.[11]

Ross and others have also made proposals to use the incentives for professional development provided by the salary systems of many school districts. These systems make a significant part of a teacher's salary dependent on accumulated educational credits. Currently, there is little restriction on what additional training is sought, and many feel that much of the training is distinctly marginal in terms of teaching performance. Reforms that sharpened the incentives of teachers to develop the skills needed in technology-rich (and other learner-centered) schools could further support the needs for staff training.

Requirements for new staff positions, such as technology coordinators or lead teachers that work with classroom teachers, can, to some degree, be met by redefining existing staff positions. The schools represented at our workshop often operated in this fashion. A teacher was designated as a part-time technology coordinator. Teachers decided to accept slightly larger classes to free one person for the role of technology coordinator. Schools, given adequate levels of autonomy with the use of their staff, can make important reallocations of staff responsibilities.

However, the marginal tapping of all these sources will defray only a part of the total resource requirements for a technology-intensive school. Given that 93 percent of the resources at the school-building level are devoted to salaries and benefits, assuming that there are limited opportunities for further pruning of noninstructional costs, and assuming that there will be little addition to overall revenues beyond that needed to accommodate additional students, some substitution of technology costs for personnel costs will be required.

---

[11]RAND has made a limited examination of these sources of funds in three districts in its work for the New American Schools Development Corporation. See Ross, unpublished.

Discussions of both the means and the probability of actually making such substitutions are beyond the scope of this report, but several "facts" are relevant. Over the past 25 years, the nation has steadily reduced the ratio of students to teachers from 25.8 to one to 17.6 to one. This is shown in Figure 4.3. This decline appears largely to be due to the addition of a significant number of teachers who serve special needs and populations, including students requiring special and remedial education or bilingual education.[12] These classes are often held in separate settings. Thus, the school class sizes reported

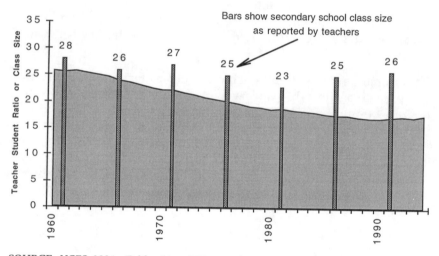

SOURCE: NCES, 1994a, Tables 64 and 69.

Figure 4.3—Decline in Pupil-Teacher Ratios over Time

[12]Richard Rothstein and Karen Miles have recently examined differences in the allocation of resources for K–12 education between 1967 and 1991. Their analysis provides a consistent but more detailed confirmation that most of the increases in teachers have been devoted to special education, education of the disadvantaged, and other functions than decreasing the class size in general education. Rothstein and Miles, 1995.

by teachers have not declined significantly over the same period as shown by the bars in the figure.[13]

As we have noted, technology provides the opportunity to significantly tailor instructional experiences to individual students. In the schools represented at the RAND workshop, teachers had regrouped themselves, and class periods had been changed. In such settings, the meaning of class size becomes blurred. Some activities may involve 40 students with one teacher in a group activity; others may involve three or four students working closely with a single teacher. Some will involve small groups of students working collaboratively with coaching from a single teacher; others will involve a student working intensively with a computer, largely on his or her own. It seems not only possible but desirable that schools integrating extensive technology into their programs review how personnel are used and even whether substituting technology or technical assistance for some personnel will lead to a more effective school.

Such changes are very difficult to make. They involve individual careers, the imperatives of the teachers' union, and beliefs of parents. Because the reallocations should occur at individual schools, it is important that those schools have substantial autonomy, either through explicit grants of authority or by the use of waivers to state and local regulations and rules. Successful budget reallocations require skillful and participatory management at the school-building level and a scope of interaction with parents at the school that has proven difficult to achieve in the past.[14]

Opportunities for Federal and State Action

The primary message of this chapter is that financing both the initial and continuing costs of incorporating technology into schools is a

---

[13]The sources of the data in Figure 4.3 are not comparable. The teacher-pupil ratios come from the Common Core Data Set, which is a census collection. The class sizes are reported in a sample survey done by the National Education Association. The picture they paint, however, is consistent with that painted by long-term teachers with whom we have talked.

[14]Researchers associated with the Consortium for Policy Research in Education (CPRE) have discussed the prerequisites for the decentralization of authority in school systems that is needed to achieve effective, restructured technology-rich schools.

local and state responsibility. Decisions concerning how to use technology and obtain required resources must be made close to the schools if support for technology is to become accepted as a normal cost of operations. Continuing reliance on special, add-on funds will delay this acceptance.

Moreover, it is likely that substantially more ubiquitous use of technology will profoundly affect the roles and work of school staffs. Such use should involve trade-offs among expenditures for equipment, software, connections to data resources, and personnel. Consequently, success in making transitions to technology-rich learning environments will require active participation by local school staffs in deciding how to acquire and use that technology. State and federal agencies can help in a variety of ways, but the fundamental direction together with the engagement of the public must rest with schools and school districts.

While local schools and districts may have the most important long-term roles, state systems have accepted and continue to play important roles. Particularly for early adopters, risks for schools are high—risks to their reputations and to the careers of their staff and the welfare of the students. It is unlikely that many restructured schools can be created without states and localities aggregating resources and making them available for the effort, as many already have.

States and larger local jurisdictions should consider setting up investment funds to support the initial development of technology-rich schools. Continued funding for operations, maintenance, and replacement should be built into the individual school's budget. These schools should also be expected to use their staff development resources to support the development of teaching skills appropriate to technology-rich learning environments.

Many states have played and are likely to continue to play important roles in seeing that schools are connected to useful information infrastructures. Some have encouraged their public utility commissions to see that all schools can have access to the national information infrastructure at a reasonable cost.

Finally, if the federal government decides to provide categorical funding for the initial startup of technology-rich schools, it is critical that such funds be provided in ways that strongly encourage schools and school systems to incorporate the continuing costs of maintaining and replacing equipment in their budgets. Federal funding for demonstrations of school programs using advanced technology and funding to schools serving special populations to support the acquisition and use of technology should, in our view, receive the highest priority. The Department of Education's research and assistance arms should also collect and disseminate information on exemplary financing practices.

PROVIDING TEACHERS WITH SKILLS NEEDED FOR EFFECTIVE TECHNOLOGY-RICH SCHOOLS

Successful use of technology in schools depends upon the skills of the teachers and other staff in those schools. Unfortunately, as participants in the RAND/CTI workshop on technology and teacher professional development put it, "professional development as currently conceived and delivered—one-shot seminars, an afternoon with an expert, or 200 teachers in a gymnasium—will not bring the profession up to speed with emerging school reforms."[15] Moreover, not only is teacher continuing professional development shallow, but there is broad consensus that the preparation of people to enter teaching is deficient as well.[16] Increasingly widespread use of technology in schools requires changes in both preservice and in-service training and, more generally, reform of policies that govern the professional development of teachers. In these changes, technology has two roles: It is the object of skill development (teachers and staff must learn to apply technology effectively for teaching and learning) and it is a means of developing skills (technology can deliver information and training).

The Nature of the Current Teaching Force

In 1991, the nation had 2.6 million public school teachers. Over 64 percent of these teachers had 10 or more years of experience in

---

[15]Harvey and Purnell, 1995, p. 1.

[16]A brief review of the recent critiques of preservice education and of proposals for its reform is contained in OTA, 1995, pp. 167–181.

teaching (Figure 4.4). About 20 percent of these teachers were 50 or older.[17]

The turnover in teachers is concentrated at the extremes of the experience distribution. Some 17 percent of the teachers with less than one year of experience left teaching in or following the 1990–91 school year.[18] This figure fell to 2.4 percent for teachers with 10 to 19 years of experience. The largest percentage of those that quickly leave the profession appear to do so because of family or personal moves, pregnancy or child-rearing, or health reasons.[19] This group forms a pool of potential teachers that often reenter teaching later in their professional lives.

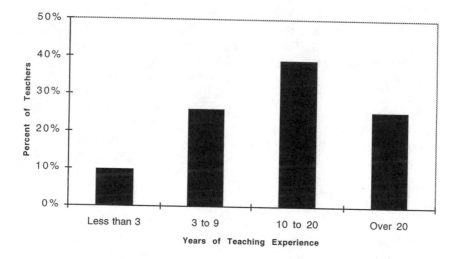

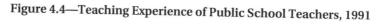

SOURCE: NCES, 1994a, Table 67.

Figure 4.4—Teaching Experience of Public School Teachers, 1991

---

[17]NCES, 1994a, Table 67.

[18]This may have been an unusually high figure; 11 percent of those with less than a year's teaching experience left teaching the year before.

[19]In 1988–89, 45 percent of teachers with three years of experience or less gave this as a reason. Only 6 percent said they were leaving because they were dissatisfied with teaching, while about 15 percent said they left for other career opportunities. NCES, 1993, Table 3.18.

Judging from the experience of the early 1990s, increasing proportions of the new hires in schools are first-time teachers. (See Table 4.1) Of the new hires in 1990–91, nearly 42 percent were first-time teachers, while a third were transfers from other schools or school districts.[20] Twenty-four percent were reentrants to teaching. In contrast, in 1987–88, about a third of the new hires were transfers, while only 31 percent were first-time teachers. Most (about 60 percent) first-time teachers in 1991–92 were fresh out of college.

The number of public school teachers is expected to grow over the coming decade. The National Center for Education Statistics projects that there will be nearly 2.8 million public school teachers by 2000 and over 2.9 million five years later.[21] On the basis of data such as these, the Office of Technology Assessment suggests that two million teachers will need to be hired over the next decade and that a high proportion will be newly trained teachers.

It is difficult to pin down the level of computer literacy possessed by the current population of teachers. It has often been said to be low, but two years ago, a survey commissioned by the National Teachers Association found that 54 percent of teachers had access to computers in their home.[22] Moreover, according to the same National Education Association survey, 65 percent of the teachers rated their computer skills as good or excellent. No doubt the majority of the younger new entrants to teaching will have used computers in schools and colleges and feel reasonably comfortable with them.

Table 4.1

**Sources of Newly Hired Teachers in Public Schools,
1988 and 1991**

Source of Supply	1988	1991
First-time teachers	30.6	41.7
Transfers from other schools	36.6	34.3
Reentrants	32.8	24.0

SOURCE: NCES, 1994b, p. 158.

---

[20]NCES, 1994b, p. 158.

[21]NCES, 1995c, Table 32. We have used the "middle alternative projection."

[22]Princeton Survey Research Associates, 1993.

However, for the technology-enabled learning environments represented by the schools described in Chapter Two, many additional skills are required. In such environments, teachers would be expected to recurrently assess student progress, create learning opportunities appropriate to the student, access resources needed for projects, and relate diverse instructional activities to the school's educational goals. By the testimony of school reformers and the individuals who attended the RAND workshops, comparatively few teachers have been prepared to perform these functions. Successful implementation of technology-enabled schools depends upon the capability to help existing teachers, as well as new entrants to the profession, to develop the skills required to perform these functions effectively.

Support for Continuing Professional Development

The RAND/CTI workshops on professional development and technology-assisted effective schooling provided insights concerning the development of the skills teachers need to possess to carry out their functions in increasingly learner-centered schooling. The workshops seem to suggest at least three common requirements for successful support of teachers moving to create these new learning environments:

1. Adequate time (and organization of time) for teachers to acquire skills and to plan the school's program and activities.

2. Assistance that is keyed to the needs of the teachers and administrators and provided at the times when they need it.

3. A clear vision concerning the purposes and the educational goals that guide the program of the school and classroom.

In the following paragraphs we highlight each of the three requirements briefly.

Adequate Time. Teachers engaged in reform universally complain about the shortage of time in which to develop the plans and new skills needed. The problem is that many of those skills must be learned at the same time teachers are carrying out their teaching functions. Many of the reforms enabled by technology require collaboration among teachers rather than simply allowing teachers to make the changes in the isolation of their own classrooms. If ways cannot be found to provide collective time for such activities without it all being done on the teachers "own" time, it is unlikely that the reforms we are discussing can take place.

Blackstock Junior High School in Port Hueneme, California, took a quite unique approach to this issue. Eight years ago, a history teacher was given a year off from teaching and told to develop a year-long history program that made significant use of technology. He was given considerable freedom and resources to allow him to redesign his classroom into what the school now calls a "smart classroom." Later, several other teachers were given the same opportunity. The initial effort appears to have been program or class centered as opposed to emphasizing the entire school.

While this may be an exemplary way in which to provide teachers with the time to learn about and develop applications of technology, a look at the cost figures in the previous section suggests that this approach is almost certainly not feasible on a large scale. More cost-effective ways of providing teachers time and skills to innovate must be found.

Northbrook Middle School in Houston, Texas, provides a different example. In a newly opening school, the principal was chosen a year in advance and had considerable latitude in choosing staff that shared her vision. Two weeks were provided all teachers to prepare during the summer before school opened.[23] The school schedule was substantially restructured to provide planning periods for teams of teachers working closely together and for staff development days. The district does provide training and support, and teachers are encouraged to attend conferences. Teachers spend time on planning and learning skills before and after school.

The Apple Classroom of Tomorrow Teacher Development Center project makes the provision of time for development of skills and plans a key requirement for participation. In addition to providing a

_____

[23]New teachers joining school must agree to spend two days in training (without compensation) before they start at the school.

teacher the time to attend week-long practicums and/or four-week summer institutes, a principal must agree to

- provide teachers with the authority and flexibility to adjust daily instructional schedules and to develop curriculum objectives that promote team teaching and interdisciplinary instruction

- allow time each day for teachers to meet and plan

- provide time for teachers to reflect on their practice

- acknowledge the importance of the team's efforts to the rest of the staff.[24]

Each of these three efforts is developmental, and thus it is obvious that teachers must have time during the development to acquire the new skills they need. However, workshop participants and others argue that this is not just a one-time requirement at the beginning of the implementation of a restructured school or program. The restructuring should provide continued time for teachers to plan and reflect and to develop professionally. Obviously, planning for professional development must also provide for new teachers at a school to develop the skills needed to function and succeed in that school.

Responsive Assistance. The attendees at the workshop on professional development emphasized the importance of assistance that is timely and keyed to the needs of teachers rather than the convenience of assistance-providing institutions or the central office. The same has been regularly emphasized by teachers implementing NASDC designs. Preparation of teachers in NASDC-related schools places a great deal of emphasis on the value of coaching—provision of assistance in situ so that teachers can relate lessons to their specific situations. (In some NASDC designs, this preparation is provided by a trained coordinator, who either is a part of the school's staff or is a frequent visitor to the school.)

Both workshop participants and teachers in the NASDC schools strongly emphasized the limitations of traditional approaches to in-service activities that do not effectively meet the needs of teachers and school staff in a timely way when those needs arise. Some be-

----

[24]Ringstaff, Marsh, and Yocum, 1995, p. 6.

lieve that technology, in the form of interactive media or a network of practitioner experts, can be effective in providing timely and relevant assistance. However, aside from the numerous on-line networks that enable practitioners to ask for and provide advice, we have found no extensive examples of such activities. While wide-band communications and multimedia materials may be able to provide timely support to teachers at some time in the future, perhaps more practical approaches involve development of the capabilities and ethos to allow teachers to support one another in a school.[25]

Individuals filling the emerging role of technology coordinator may be able to play an important role in the development of their colleagues. We have heard from several school leaders that technology coordinators sometimes do play an important role in demonstrating effective technology-enabled pedagogical strategies and in coaching teachers in the effective use of technology. However, it appears that this is not a very common practice. Becker, in his analysis of the 1992 IEA data, reports on the distribution of effort of what he terms major coordinators.[26] His findings are shown in Table 4.2. Clearly, training and helping teachers is not a major function for most of the coordinators surveyed. Teaching and supervising students using computers occupies an average 54 percent of their time. Help to teachers averages 3.6 hours of effort per week.

Professional Development Responding to Educational Vision and Goals. Perhaps the importance of a clear, school-level educational vision and goal seems peripheral to the issue of professional development, but it seemed very important to the school representatives attending the RAND workshop on technology-assisted effective schooling. Computers, communications, and video can make a day's experience in a classroom fun. Kids can be deeply engaged. The idea that teachers should be guides to or co-learners with students is ap-

---

[25]A study commissioned by the Office of Technology Assessment provides case studies of two districts that have technology programs fostering such activities. See the case studies on Bellevue, Washington, and Jefferson County, Kentucky, in Beryl Buck Institute for Education, 1994.

[26]"'Major coordinators' are those who either spent at least 20 hours per week in activities related to this position or for whom the position of computer coordinator constituted at least 50 percent of their responsibilities." Becker, 1994, Table 7.4.

Table 4.2

Activities of School-Level Technology Coordinators, 1992

Activities	Hours	Mean Percentage of Effort
Teach, supervise students using computers	19.5	54
Train, help teachers to use computers	3.6	9
Select and acquire material, equipment	2.3	6
Maintain equipment and software	4.0	11
Self-development	4.0	11
Other (write software, lesson plans, all other)	4.1	11
Total number of hours per week	37.5	

NOTE: Percentages in final column are means of the responses for the activity. Data are for those categorized as "major coordinators."
SOURCE: Becker, 1994, Table 7.4.

pealing. Moreover, many implementations of technology in classrooms and schools have heavy leadership from technologists or developers who visualize exciting opportunities made possible by the infusion of new technologies, software, or communications.

The danger is that these exciting things will not add up to anything. The student may develop some deep knowledge about one subject area or an enthusiasm for a classroom activity that is exciting, but parents and the community are left with the uncomfortable feeling that the fundamental skills and knowledge that they believe kids should have are not being imparted.

Each of the schools that made presentations to the workshop appeared to have a clear educational sense of purpose. Technology served that purpose. The professional development of teachers served that purpose. The Christopher Columbus school derived its guidance from an extensive systemwide effort to create a curriculum framework emphasizing a "whole language philosophy of education." This starting point led to revamping the schedule of the school day, the introduction of more cross-curricular thematic units, support for professional development, and as a final step, the integration of technology into school activity. The district and school administration made it clear that this last step was a means to the curricular ends that they had established.

The Taylorsville school represented a distinctive, school-centered approach to the development of a technology-enabled school. As we noted in the last chapter, it is an elementary school affiliated with the Modern Red School House design activity (MRSH) funded by NASDC. Its efforts to transform itself started with a set of standards for student learning that MRSH has developed that derive from the various national standards development efforts. These standards, which may be modified somewhat by the requirements of the district or state (Indiana), provide guidance to the curriculum development, the assessments, and the sequencing of activities in the school. The standards are built into a computer-based instructional management system that supports the refinement of the curriculum as well as student learning contracts that are intended to provide the individualization that is sought in the school design. The design implementation requires teachers to develop curriculum units as a means to professional development. The design also seeks to develop the skills of teachers as members of the governance structure of the schools. Altogether, the professional development activities of the school staff are guided by an overall vision and goals inherent in the MRSH design.

In sum, as illustrated by these two examples, a reformed and restructured school (whether or not it uses technology) must have a clear sense of its educational mission that is shared by its staff, its students, and its parents. The professional development required of its staff must, in turn, be guided by the functional needs associated with the vision, together with the existing capabilities of the teachers. An important implication is that the details of professional development activities should be shaped by individual schools rather than by a school system's central office.

Preservice Training for Teachers

The emphasis in our meetings was clearly on the continuing professional development of teachers who were already in schools. However, over the coming decade a significant number of newly trained teachers will enter the nation's schools. The training of these new teachers should impart skills and attitudes that will allow these teachers to function effectively in technology-enabled learning environments. This is far more than a matter of ensuring that they possess the skills needed to use computers and other equipment, and it requires fundamental changes in the curriculum of most colleges and changes in the accreditation requirements for teachers.

The recent OTA report on teachers and technology reviewed activities of colleges of education and painted a fairly discouraging picture of their capabilities to make such changes.[27] The difficulties faced by these schools are systemic and related to their place in higher education generally. OTA suggests that these difficulties stem from a lack of access to resources, faculty attitudes and training, and lack of institutional support for work with technology. However, the reform and restructuring of these institutions is much broader than that required by the increasing importance of technology and beyond the scope of this report.

On the other hand, the OTA report does catalogue a number of experiments by schools of education using technology that provide a rather rich picture of the potential technology has as both a means for fulfilling traditional missions in more effective ways and as an agent for fostering college of education reforms. The examples, which have required substantial funding over sustained periods of time, suggest the potential fruitfulness of research and development expenditures in this area.

Opportunities for Federal, State, and Local Action[28]

The preceding discussion suggests that teachers' and administrators' greatest problems are not with learning to use technology but instead with learning to develop and manage the types of learning environments that are facilitated by these technologies. Judging from the experience of the schools that participated in our workshop, as well as explicit professional development activities such as the ACOT Teacher Development Centers, we believe that much of the

---

[27]OTA, 1995, Chapter 5 in general and pp. 187–191 in particular.

[28]It should be noted that a number of national and local foundations are making important investments to help school districts develop improved professional development strategies. Among these are The Pew Charitable Trusts and The MacArthur Foundation.

best professional development occurs at work, doing work, and reflecting on the work that is done.

If this is the case, a principal task for local school districts is to make such activities possible and to provide assistance to school faculties in accordance with their needs. For many districts, this means a profound restructuring of the way in which they conduct staff development activities. It also requires a cultural change at the school-building level that leads the principal and the faculty to take greater responsibility for their professional development.

While we believe much of the action must be at the local level, there are important roles for state and federal actors as well. States play a major role shaping teacher certification requirements which, in turn, shape the programs of teacher training institutions. Working with organizations like the National Council for Accrediting of Teacher Education (NCATE), they should seek to revise certification requirements to ensure that new teachers possess skills that allow them to enter and effectively work in technology-enabled schools.

The federal government supports many programs and institutions providing assistance to teachers, schools, and school districts.[29] It also supports R&D for improved methods for training teachers and supports programs to train teachers, primarily in math and science. These programs should be periodically reviewed and encouraged to address needs posed by technology-rich learning environments as well as to use technology to enhance the delivery of training and assistance relevant to those environments.

ENSURING THAT NEEDED SOFTWARE IS AVAILABLE

Educational technology without appropriate software is of little or no use. As we conducted this study, we repeatedly heard that despite the voluminous listings of educational software titles, there was a shortage of software that teachers and others viewed as needed in schools. As a consequence, RAND sponsored two workshops devoted to the issue of educational software. These, together with the experiences of the technology-rich schools surveyed, suggest the ex-

---

[29]A list of such programs is contained in OTA, 1995, Tables 6-2 and 6-3.

isting market for educational software does not appear to provide appropriate incentives to develop all the software that is needed.

Today's technology-rich schools, as represented by the schools described in Chapter Two, rely on a spectrum of software. They use

1. drill-and-practice software developed in the past (frequently with partial federal support) and focused primarily on the needs of the elementary grades

2. curricular and pedagogical practices exploiting existing applications software (e.g., communications, word processing, or spreadsheets) coupled with access to computer-based and other content

3. reference materials that are now appearing in CD-ROM formats that are sold both to schools and homes

4. instructional management software that aids a school's staff to help all students acquire and demonstrate the skills and knowledge sought by the community

5. administrative support software such as programs supporting student grading or keeping attendance records.

In quite a few instances, individual teachers and schools have also acquired software originally developed for the home entertainment market (e.g., *Where in the World is Carmen San Diego* and *SimCity*) that they feel can help them in their classes.

The software underlying the above applications falls into three broad categories. Software "tools" are application packages similar or identical to those commonly used in offices and homes. The development of word processors and spreadsheets is driven by these larger markets, and schools use what is available. Content software incorporates information, curricular structure, and often, some form of specialized instructional management system. Common examples are the integrated learning systems (ILS) and less elaborate drill-and-practice programs. Instructional management systems are a newly emerging class of software that helps a school to relate its instructional program to the district's curriculum framework, supports the development of individual work plans for students, and tracks and displays indicators of the performance of students.

The tools software poses little problem because it relies on larger commercial markets. Some instructional management software is available and more is being developed. While school representatives at our workshop said the existing products were expensive and not yet fully suited to their needs, there was no general sense conveyed that there is a significant market problem. Workshop participants generally agreed, however, that there was a shortage of content software, particularly for middle and secondary school students.

Current technology-rich schools tend to place a good deal of emphasis on project-based learning using communications, word-processing, and spreadsheet software. As we noted earlier, this reflects the lessons of modern cognitive science concerning constructivist and situated learning as well as the long-espoused views of educational philosophers such as Dewey. In such schools (and in others sharing these views, if not the technology), individual teachers normally design the projects and must ensure that these projects produce the skills that students need to acquire. Such projects are found in virtually all subject areas, including science, math, history and social studies, and language arts—often in interdisciplinary activities.

While we are strong supporters of project-based learning, we believe that too extensive a reliance on such pedagogy may pose a significant risk for the current school reform movement. Much of the current development of such projects takes place in exceptional schools at the leading edge of school reform. The teachers involved are often among the most qualified in their schools and school systems. When expanded to many more schools, particularly to those with teachers less motivated or less well prepared, the educational benefits of this pedagogy may prove disappointing to policymakers and parents alike. Moreover, many teachers may come to resent the added burden of creating and recreating motivating projects for students. The result could be disillusionment similar to that which killed the progressive school movement in the 1930s.

A complement, and partial alternative to this use of technology, is content software that incorporates some of the structure of current textbooks but does so in a manner that engages students in a far more effective way. Such software would be sophisticated in pedagogy and rich in the imagery required to motivate the attention of today's adolescent student. Properly used, such software could help "demassify" current instruction and attend to the individual needs of each student. It can do this, in part, by freeing "learning time" from the restrictions of the rigid schedules of today's schools and extending it to other hours and places.

An illustrative example of this class of software appears in the box below.

This scenario is drawn from 'Dreamworld' by Jacob T. Schwartz, an article in the Summer 1987 issue of Daedalus, p. 170, A Lesson in Ancient History.

The student, in a college-level world history course, is reviewing the sequence of political events surrounding the collapse of the Roman Republic and the rise of the Principate of Augustus. Some of the material is presented as text, which appears on the screen in an attractive booklike format, with still illustrations occupying roughly a quarter of the screen. The text can be enlivened by occasional (optional) audio quotations from ancient sources, such as Plutarch's Lives of the Noble Romans; each of these can be delivered in the voice of an actor who represents the ancient author. This material is visually announced on the screen: "Concerning Crassus, Plutarch said the following . . . ." This line appears in a color that the student recognizes as meaning that an optional audio insert is available. If he touches this line on the screen, the video illustration on the page switches to an image of a bust of Crassus, while Plutarch's remark on Crassus is read in a voice emphasizing its drama and irony. Later in the lesson, information concerning the Battle of Philippi is presented, first by text explaining its date and significance, then by five to ten minutes of filmed material . . . introduced with a compelling musical fanfare. A map of Italy and Greece is displayed, showing the paths taken by the Republican and Antonian armies to the battle. This is followed by a more detailed map of the area of northern Greece in which the battle was fought, and by video footage of the terrain of Philippi, taken from a helicopter. After this, a brief enactment of the battle is shown, with views of its commanders in action, voice-over commentary on its main incidents, and dramatic scenes of the suicides of Cassius and Brutus. These video clips yield to text reviewing the significance of the battle and ensuing events, with audio statements from authorities on ancient history reflecting on the battle's significance for the Roman World.

The content in such a piece of software would be reinforced by a set of open-ended questions demanding an energetic line of independent inquiry (perhaps computer assisted) by the student, as in the following examples:

- What was the size of these armies by comparison to a modern army?

- How large was the civilian population to support armies of this size?

- What are typical ratios of civilian population to military personnel in wartime today, and if much different, explain the difference?

- What was the cost to maintain these standing armies and the "GNP" required to do so?

- What materials were used for weaponry and armor?

The student would be graded on the answers, on the approach to reaching them, and on the amount of assistance required from the teacher. The approach and grades would be stored in a computer file for review by parents and by other teachers, as necessary.

This is but one form of content software. There are others such as the intelligent tutors that have been developed with National Science Foundation (NSF) and other funding; simulations, which require students to examine public policy issues such as health care; and virtual environments in which students can conduct simulated scientific experiments. A well-known and quite widely used class of content software supports foreign language instruction.

Market Supply and Demand for Educational Software

As we have noted, there is a general consensus that there is too little high-quality content software. This is particularly true for the upper grade levels. There are repeated rumors that major software firms intend to develop applications for the education market. The so-called home education market is growing rapidly. There is software to coach students in taking major examinations such as the Scholastic Achievement Test (SAT). But an abundance of high-quality content software, such as we described above, has yet to appear.

To investigate the nature of the education software market, RAND held two workshops (one in November 1993 and the other in February 1995[30]) at which representatives of textbook publishers, ILS vendors, educational software publishers, and multimedia developers were present. Both workshops explored the demand for and the supply of software, with emphasis on content software. Based on information provided by the participants, we estimate that the size of the school market for software was less than $750 million in 1994; about 0.3 percent of all K-12 educational expenditures. This figure can be compared with an estimate of nearly $400 million in expenditures by households for "edutainment" and reference CD-ROMs in the first year (1994) that "home" computers were marketed with integrated CD-ROM drives. The largest fraction of sales was basic-skills software to elementary schools often in the form of large-scale, integrated learning systems costing $30,000 or more per installation.

The attendees at the workshops clarified the disincentives they face in expanding the supply of software. Traditional school textbook publishers consider that they operate in a zero-sum game, that the school budget structure sharply limits what can be spent on instructional materials of all kinds, and that any software sales they make will simply cut into their volume of textbook sales. They note too that software development costs can be high, and that even such an unambiguous marketing success as selling one software copy to each and every one of the nation's schools need not guarantee a positive return on investment.

These factors do not appear to inhibit low-overhead educational software publishers, who can successfully find a market niche for education and training materials in schools, hospitals, and prisons. Such companies have found profitable markets for materials that supplement existing textbook and other materials. They do not, however, have the capital necessary to engage in major development efforts.

New multimedia developers, whether conglomerates like Paramount or more modest independent firms like Broderbund, find the home market with its nearly 100 million households a far more appealing

---

[30]Harvey, 1995b.

target than the nation's 100 thousand schools. Even at $50 a copy, a single successful CD-ROM that sells to only 1 percent of U.S. households can produce revenues of $50 million in a relatively short time period. By contrast, if it developed a comparably priced CD-ROM for schools and sold it to *all* 100,000 of them, it would have revenues of $5 million. So while an industry is taking shape that is potentially capable[31] of meeting the school need for sophisticated content software, its output is presently directed to a more lucrative market segment.

The pioneer, technology-rich schools, whose costs we examined in Chapter Three, provide some additional hints on why the school software market is not now particularly attractive. In these schools, software expenditures ranged between 4 percent and 10 percent of total annualized technology implementation costs; about one-fifth of hardware costs. (By contrast, software costs tend to approach the value of hardware costs in typical enterprise computing.)

In their report,[32] Keltner and Ross provide a partial explanation for the low proportion of technology expenditures devoted to software:

> The school environment is not one that puts sophisticated demands on the software component of a technology program. The number of basic software programs installed on individual student computers is typically limited. None of the schools in our survey purchased site licenses for more than five to six "tool-based" software products, e.g., Microsoft Word, Clarisworks, Hypertext or Hypercard, and the average figure was more like three. With a site license for 25 computers costing between $1000 and $1500, an expenditure of $3000 to $4000 typically proved enough to outfit an entire classroom of computers with basic software applications.

Continuing with their explanation, they write,

> Another explanation for the low level of software expenditure is the ability of schools to generate economies of scale in the use of expensive "content-based" software products. The Christopher Columbus, Corona and Elizabeth St. schools each spent $30,000 to

---

[31]That is, with a capability for the necessary rich imagery, and potentially able to acquire the capabilities for sophisticated pedagogy and course content.

[32]Keltner and Ross, 1996.

$40,000 to set up large libraries of CD-ROM and laserdisk software products. While expensive, these software items do not increase software expenditures per student significantly, because their cost is distributed over a large number of classrooms. Blackstock and Taylorsville schools spent $43,000 and $70,000 respectively on network and instructional management software. Network and instructional management system software products too are also normally used on a school-wide or classroom-based LAN.

When these school-level perspectives are put together with the comparatively small number of schools and the complexity of selling to 15,000 school districts governed by all manner of adoption practices, it is easy to see why software firms that are not traditionally associated with formal education view this market with some skepticism.

To summarize, the traditional providers of instructional materials, the textbook manufacturers, are anxiously watching but apparently not ready to strike out in a big way for fear of jeopardizing current markets. The major providers of educational software, firms specializing in integrated learning systems, have developed a business based upon a low volume with high margins, which is not well adapted to developing and selling applications for individual use on large numbers of unintegrated computers. Small software firms have found profitable niches but lack the resources (and perhaps a taste for risk) needed to strike out into new developments. The new multimedia firms not only lack deep knowledge of educational needs in schools but have a production and distribution system keyed to high sales volumes with comparatively low margins. To date, the result is the "shortage" of content software reported by so many of the people with whom we have consulted.[33]

---

[33]We should note another problem with the educational technology market that has been important in the past. As we noted in Section 2, while there are many computers in the schools, they are of an immense variety of brands and vintages. Developing for multiple platforms increases costs substantially, and the fact that many of the computers lack hard drives and modern video displays limits the installed base available to a software developer. This problem is lessening with time, but as long as the Macintosh-PC distinction remains strong it will remain.

Opportunities for Federal, State, and Local Action

In a market as dynamic as educational technology, it is difficult to decide whether specific government actions will help or hinder the public interest. We have heard of potentially exciting product ideas from individual developers, but whether they can find the capital, produce a product, and overcome the marketing barriers that we have described is uncertain. Surely large firms like Microsoft, Apple, and IBM have plenty of resources and ideas; in both IBM and Apple's case they also have a substantial history of working in the K–12 education market. However, content software of the sort needed for middle and secondary schools has not been their priority.

Our discussion of financing earlier in this chapter did consider two approaches that would serve to increase demand for software and thus should promote improvements in the quantity and quality of supply. The first is the restructuring of traditional school budgets so as to raise the current proportion of the budget devoted to the acquisition of instructional materials. The second is state or public-private investment strategies for increasing the investment in technology generally and thus software expenditures as well. If such changes are made and the density of computers continues to increase significantly, the attractiveness of the market will increase correspondingly.

The major tool available to the federal government is its R&D program. As we have noted, federal R&D support was a major contributor to the early development, and hence the current availability, of drill-and-practice materials in the basic skills. Current NSF funding is providing support for potentially important content software, primarily in mathematics and science. The transfer of such developments to the private sector (where appropriate) has always been very difficult, but the magnitude of the investment suggests that explicit attention should continue to be given to the problem. It is possible too that a program of federal support for pre-competitive multimedia educational software R&D might also serve to counter market disincentives presently faced by software vendors.

Beyond this, the federal government should be looking for every chance it can to promote discussion and consultation among software developers, publishers, scholars, and educators concerning potential software applications. No one group can deal with this problem alone. At our first workshop, attendees suggested that a joint public-private institute be founded, one of whose major purposes would be to support just such discussions. Such an institution would hold regular symposia for developers and educators, maintain databases of exemplary technology applications, foster the development of technical standards, and generally serve as a clearinghouse and convener. Whether such an institution could capture the support of the members of a potentially highly competitive industry is a question that would have to be answered before serious consideration is devoted to its establishment.

Chapter Five

SUMMARY AND CONCLUSIONS

This report has sought to take stock of the current status of the use of technology by the nation's public elementary and secondary schools and to suggest some of the challenges that face educators, policymakers, and producers of educational technology and software as they seek to expand and deepen the use of technology in schools. In this final chapter, we summarize our findings and suggest the broad elements of a national strategy for moving forward. That strategy is predicated on the fact that the school use of technology is already expanding at a significant rate and that the technology itself is evolving rapidly. We conclude by discussing the roles that the federal government should play in a national strategy facilitating the most effective use of technology by schools and students.

FINDINGS

1. *Educational technology has significant potential for improving students' learning.*

Both research and the experience of practitioners suggest that, properly implemented, technology can support improved student learning. Most of this research and experience has dealt with small, individual applications of technology. However, a small proportion of the nation's schools have intensively and effectively implemented a variety of educational technologies in ways that engage and motivate students to achieve performance levels and improvements consistent with the nation's educational goals. They have done this by using technology to

- tailor learning experiences more clearly to learner needs and abilities

- provide students with access to resources and expertise outside the school

- support more authentic assessment of a student's progress

- manage and guide the learning activities of the students.

On the basis of the experience of these schools, and of numerous smaller, less systemic applications of technology, we conclude that the modern reform agenda for schools, particularly that part of the agenda dealing with providing an instructional program that enables all students to meet challenging standards, can be strongly supported by technology. Indeed, we think this agenda may not be achievable without the use of technology to support the functions outlined above.

2. *Extensive use of technology in schools has the potential to promote significant school restructuring and expand the time and motivation for student learning.*

We share the view of Louis Gerstner, quoted in the first chapter of this report: "[Information technology] is the force that revolutionizes business, streamlines government and enables instant communications and the exchange of information among people and institutions around the world." However, few schools (or school systems) have had the levels of technology required to support such restructuring, fewer have had technology long enough for restructuring to have been fully worked out, and most efforts have not been extensively documented.

Nonetheless, existing research and the experience of the pioneer schools we consulted are promising and suggestive. Students, teachers, and administrators report taking new roles. Technology has been used as an instructional management tool. Students and their parents report they are more motivated. There is some evidence of improvement on traditional measures of student outcome.

However, the evidence from these schools must be put into an appropriate context. These schools, as early adopters of technology, are clearly exceptional. Moreover, the concepts of learning and instruction that these schools have used are not new. They have foundations in the work of Dewey, in the progressive school movement, and in the modern findings of cognitive scientists. These concepts are also intuitively appealing and, in the hands of skilled practitioners, have proven effective. However, past reform movements built on these concepts have foundered. Systemic barriers—inadequately trained teachers, the lack of clearly defined standards, the effort required to manage many independent student learning activities, and lack of success in gaining broad public support—prevented high performance and widespread adoption.

Technology has the potential to deal with some of these past problems. It can support the management of complex, standards-related instructional processes in ways that have previously been achieved by only the most skilled teachers. It can facilitate communications among teachers so they can collaborate more effectively. Technology can also promote communications among schools, students, and parents that fosters greater accountability and public support.

The potential for success may also be improved because technology is being introduced into schools in a time of broader, systemic reform. The development of clearer and higher standards and associated assessments, a major objective of the systemic reform movement, can sharpen the understanding of a community's goals for education and can sharpen the performance of schools in meeting those goals. Standards and assessments should provide a necessary discipline to a community's schools. At the same time, schools of education, state accreditation agencies, and school systems are being urged to rethink and align their programs with high standards.

But it is important to reiterate that while the early experience with pioneer, technology-rich schools appears promising, it remains to be seen whether technology-rich learning environments can be implemented in large numbers of schools with comparable outcomes.

3. *The growth in use of technology by schools is strong; schools are adding equipment and developing connections to the national information infrastructure at a high rate. However, many schools still lack significant access to technology.*

Chapter Two documented the rapid expansion in the levels of technology in schools. This expansion is projected to continue at rates that are substantially in excess of the rate of growth of overall school expenditures. The motivation for expanded use of technology is most often to provide students with skills in the use of technology that are central to today's and tomorrow's workplace. For some school systems, the investments are also motivated by a desire to enrich instructional programs of schools with distance learning or access to educationally relevant resources on various wide-area networks.

Despite this rapid growth, data in Chapter Two suggest that the average school still makes limited use of computers and substantial numbers of schools have very limited access to technology of any kind. The uses espoused by advocates of technology-supported instruction are comparatively rare and limited to individual teachers who are excited by the potential that they feel technology has to motivate their students or to access new resources.

4. *Data from a study by the IEA in 1992 suggested the availability of technology in schools serving poor, minority, and special needs populations did not appear to lag substantially behind the averages of schools taken as a whole. However, to the extent that technology enables learning outside the school, large disparities in the access of students of different classes and ethnicity to technology is a matter of concern.*

Past federal, state, and local funding and policies appear to have mitigated extreme differences in the average availability of computers among special populations. In particular, federal compensatory education programs have supported the acquisition of substantial technology for schools serving disadvantaged populations, particularly at the elementary levels. While this was the case during the 1992–93 time period during which most of the data we use was collected, it is less clear what has and will happen as larger proportions of funding for technology are drawn from state and local (as opposed to federal) sources.

In contrast, the disparities in home possession and use of computers are substantial among families with differing incomes, parental education, and ethnicity.[1] To the degree that technology comes to be

_____

[1]These statistics are summarized in Chapter 2 of Anderson et al., 1995.

used to extend the amount of time spent in learning activities outside the schools, these disparities could have considerable consequences for the achievements of students from different family backgrounds. If the disparities persist, access to technology is likely to become one more element in an array of factors that cause a student's educational attainment to be highly correlated with the socioeconomic status of his or her family.

5.   *Some schools and school districts have moved rapidly to a fairly ubiquitous use of technology, and their experiences should provide guidance to others that are following.*

The penetration of any innovation into a population tends to follow a familiar "s-shaped" curve in which some members of the population are early adopters, most are follow-on adopters, and a few lag far behind in adoptions. This is the case with technology in both school districts and schools. A few districts are well out ahead of the general population of districts in the numbers of computers they are providing to their students or the completeness of the networking of their schools. Similarly, as we have seen, there are some schools that now have a computer for nearly every student in the school. These early adopters constitute a rich source of information concerning the acquisition and use of technology.

6.   *The costs of ubiquitous use of technology are modest in the context of overall budgets for public elementary education but moving to such use requires significant and potentially painful restructuring of budgets.*

The estimated annualized costs related to technology use in the schools examined by Keltner and Ross for this report ranged from about $180 to $450 per student. In 1994–95 the current expenditure per student in average daily attendance was $5,623. If we take $300 as a plausible target level of funding per student for technology-related costs, about 5.3 percent of the budgets of schools would need to be allocated to technology. On its face, this seems a level that should be attainable.

However, our estimate of actual expenditures per student in 1994–95 is $70, or one quarter of the $300 figure. The bulk of school budgets are devoted to personnel costs; in most districts, funding for materials and supplies is very restricted and provides little opportunity for further reallocation to technology. Supporting levels of expenditure equal to $300 per pupil will consequently require reallocations of funds that have proven very difficult to achieve in public schools and/or increments in funding that taxpayers in most jurisdictions have been reluctant to provide. Such reallocation will be possible only if the public and the educational community come to feel that technology is essential to meeting their objectives for student learning. Information about and demonstration of the importance of technology are essential to continued growth in technology's use.

7.   *When technology is deeply infused in a school's operations, teachers tend to assume new roles and require new skills. There is a strong consensus among the experts we consulted that neither the initial preparation of teachers nor the current strategies for continued professional development have been effective in developing these skills.*

The practices of the pioneer schools we examined as well as the testimony of experts point strongly to the need for changes not only in the substance of education courses and training programs but for changes in the manner in which teachers use their time. More time to critically review the teaching practices of others, to collaborate on the development of courses, and to work collaboratively on the assessment of student work will contribute both to the quality of the instructional program and to the professional development of teachers.

8.   *While there has been a rapid expansion in home education software, the market for school-based content software has been modest and comparatively stagnant. Quality content software for middle and secondary schools is not broadly available. However, this market is likely to evolve rapidly.*

As noted in Chapter Four, the school-based market for educational software has grown somewhat in recent years but has been stagnant compared with the growth in home education or "edutainment" software. Moreover, the bulk of the school-based content software has been prepared for the elementary grade levels and has emphasized the development of basic skills.

Experts vary in their assessment of the importance of the shortage in content software. Some feel that the use of software tools (e.g., word processors and spreadsheets) coupled with network-based information resources will come to be the norm. To them content software per se has relatively little importance. Others argue that content software, keyed to emerging standards, is an important component of the technology-rich school of the future because teachers need the expertise and wisdom that can be built into content software (as it has been built into textbooks in the past).

The market for educational materials, as traditionally structured, offers limited incentives for entrepreneurial development of content software. The market is fragmented and governed by a variety of materials adoption practices. Even if a high proportion of schools acquire a product, the volume of sales is small. This is particularly true with the more specialized subject areas characteristic of much of secondary education.

The traditional sources of instructional content, the textbook publishers, have seen this market as "zero-sum." Gains in software sales would be offset by losses in textbook sales. Unless faced with the loss of their markets to new competitors, they have few incentives to actively develop software. Companies specializing in multimedia have focused on the home market where they hope for large volumes of sales and low margins.

However, the nature of this market has the potential to change rapidly. As the density of computers in schools increases, content software may become more critical and demand may increase. Alliances between traditional publishers and newer multimedia companies are being formed with the hope of exploiting synergy between the school and home markets. The likely expansion of software distribution via the Internet will reduce distribution costs and may serve to aggregate the market.

ELEMENTS OF A NATIONAL STRATEGY TO EXPAND THE USE OF TECHNOLOGY IN EDUCATION

Educational technology is currently an area of vibrant development. Technology is being acquired at an historically high rate. New firms or partnerships among existing firms are emerging in an attempt to exploit a market thought to lurk in a $250 billion enterprise. Networks of teachers and other school professionals are active and proliferating. Public-private partnerships are being formed to wire schools or assist in the broader implementation of educational technology. In the midst of all this activity, is there a need for a strategy or at least some strategic principles that might guide the numerous actors that are now so actively engaged?

In our view some sense of strategy is needed to overcome the problems seen in past efforts to promote the use of technology and reform in the nation's schools. All too frequently, past efforts foundered because implementation was flawed, communities and teachers were not adequately involved, or inadequate resources were devoted to the task. Some attention to these lessons will help the nation increase the probability that investments in technology will yield improved outcomes in terms of student learning.

A full strategy is surely too ambitious. Gaining agreement from key actors in all sectors would be difficult or impossible. Revising the strategy in the face of rapid changes in technology would be impossibly cumbersome. However, we propose several principles to guide the nation as it moves to introduce additional information technology into its schools. These principles are simple and straightforward—intended to shape an ongoing activity rather than spur new activities.

1.   The introduction of educational technology into schools should occur as a component of a broader effort of school reform to improve the learning of all children.

2.   Over time, the recurring costs of educational technology should be built into school budgets as a normal component of recurring costs. Major responsibility for financing and implementing technology clearly lies with state and local school authorities.

3.   Public authorities at all levels should work with the private sector to see that all schools have access to the national information infrastructure at reasonable costs.

4.   All levels of government should monitor the access to technology that exists for traditionally disadvantaged populations and be prepared to do what is possible to ensure equality of access.

5. All levels of government should seek to learn and use the lessons from schools and school districts that pioneer in the creation of technology-rich learning environments.

6. The federal government's role should involve leadership, funding of research and development, dissemination of information on effective practice, and managing existing programs in ways that capitalize on the benefits of educational technology.

We treat each of these very briefly and then, in our final subsection, deal more extensively with the role of the federal government.

Relate Use of Technology to Educational Reform Agenda

It is clearly possible to create a modest number of technology-rich schools across the country by treating each as an exception to normal operations in a district. This is the way the pioneer schools we examined were created, and it is the way that most model schools are treated. However, the goal is ultimately to make technology-rich schools the norm and for these schools to assist all their students to perform well against standards set by their state and community. For this to occur, the other components of reform must be carried through as well. Standards and related assessments are needed; curriculum frameworks should be in place to guide school-level professionals; professional development opportunities must be readily available and of high quality; and schools need the autonomy to allocate resources to meet the needs of their students. Reform efforts related to many of these issues are under way across the nation, and effective use of technology should be a part of them.

We have argued that technology itself can be an important catalyst for change. While a rational approach to school improvement might say "figure out what you want to do before you acquire the materials, training, and technology to do it," this is too often a recipe for the status quo or marginal change. Ubiquitous and networked technology can create instructional opportunities at the school level that lead to changes not imagined ahead of time. Technology can foster communications among teachers, students, parents, and administrators that change perceptions of what a school should be doing and how it should be doing it. Reform in some schools can start with the acquisition of technology.

Build Costs of Educational Technology into State and Local Education Budgets

If technology is to become a regular and integral component of elementary and secondary education, its costs must come to be seen as a regular cost of doing business. If a program is treated as an add-on, as is the case when it is supported by external, categorical grants, experience has shown that it is unlikely to become deeply incorporated in a school and to survive the withdrawal of the grant. A nation of technology-rich schools cannot be built with special-purpose, categorical funding.

This is not to say that such funding is not an appropriate way to begin. The experiences of Kentucky, Ohio, Texas, and North Carolina, to mention but a few states, are testimony to the importance of the kick start leading to more technology-rich schools provided by special appropriations for technology.

Provide Access to National Information Infrastructure

We cannot predict what many future uses of information technology in education will be. However, the explosive growth of a wide spectrum of applications such as E-mail and the World Wide Web makes it clear that routine use of the national information infrastructure is likely. Schools should participate in this use.

The emerging information and communications infrastructure is and will be dominated by commercial interests. Its future shape will be guided by commercial incentives. Schools and other community institutions such as libraries, museums, and social service agencies may not have the financial clout to shape the infrastructure in ways that serve their needs. In creating whatever regulatory and market structure that guides the evolution of the infrastructure, public officials at all levels should be mindful of these needs.

Monitor the Equality of Access to Benefits of Educational Technology and Work to Improve That Equality of Access Where Possible

Much has been written concerning the information haves and have-nots. Some, with visions of a future in which access to and the ability to use information are critical to personal success, seek assurances that effective, universal access to the national information infrastructure be guaranteed. Others are less certain that access to information will be crucial to everyone or about how the infrastructure will evolve. They do not feel a forceful public response is needed now.

Evidence suggests that while there is some inequality in the access possessed by disadvantaged relative to more advantaged populations, it is less than the inequality that exists between large and small schools or between some states. That there are not greater inequalities is almost certainly the result of past public policy, particularly the federal policies governing the allocation of Department of Education funding.

School-level access varies less than access in homes. To the extent that the out-of-school use of technology assumes greater importance in the learning of students, this large disparity should be of considerable public concern. Historically, it has been comparatively easy for federal and state policy to at least partially correct for resource inequalities in schools. It is far more problematic whether such policies can compensate for unequal effective access outside schools.

We do not advocate immediate actions to deal with unequal access to educational technology. We do feel that there is a good chance that such inequality of access could develop into a significant concern for a nation that has traditionally been committed to equality of educational opportunity. In our discussion of appropriate federal activities, we will propose both monitoring this issue and R&D on ways in which to compensate for unequal access.

Capitalize on the Lessons of Pioneer Schools and Districts

There are pioneer schools and school districts that have moved rapidly to introduce and exploit technology. These sites provide a unique opportunity to learn from experience. Because of the need for high-quality information concerning the effectiveness and implementation of technology-rich schools, we propose that the federal government develop a program to monitor these activities for the lessons that they hold.

The Federal Role in Fostering Effective Use of Educational Technology

While the major burdens for acquiring and using educational technology lie with schools, school systems, and states, there are important (and quite traditional) roles the federal government should play. These encompass four major classes of activities.

1. Continuing advocacy and leadership for school reform, emphasizing the potential that technology has for improving student performance.

2. Creating and disseminating high-quality information concerning the effective deployment and use of education technology.

3. Fostering the development of assistance organizations that will help schools and school systems successfully implement effective, technology-enabled schools.

4. Sustaining a vigorous and relevant program of research and development related to educational technology.

Leadership and Advocacy. The president, vice president, and Secretary of Education have provided significant visibility to the opportunities offered by educational technology and by a more effective national information infrastructure. They have had much to do with the current excitement about educational technology. They have provided this leadership within a broad reform framework worked out over a decade by the governors, the president, and others from the executive branch, the business community, Congress, and educational leaders.

The framework builds on the national educational goals adopted by the governors and President Bush in 1989 and amended by the Goals 2000 legislation in 1994. It encourages the development and use of high academic standards by states and localities. Many states and communities have moved forward to create such standards and to develop assessment systems that will help schools and school districts to gauge their performance. The Goals 2000 legislation, along with the reauthorization of the Elementary and Secondary Education Act (now called the Improving America's Schools Act), reshaped a number of federal programs and authorized several new programs that are intended to help states and localities reform their schools to meet the national goals.

In our view, the framework is sound. However, as this was being written, the Congress and the executive branch were locked in a major debate about the future of many federal programs and initiatives and about the appropriate federal role in education. Whatever the resolution of this debate, we expect there will remain important leadership roles and functions for the federal government and its officers. Two seem particularly fruitful—convening public and private officials who share common problems and identifying and recognizing examples of outstanding individual and school performance.

Even in these times of political turbulence and change, most Americans look to leaders of the federal government for guidance. Thus the federal government can bring state and local leaders, executives of private firms, community leaders, or representatives of key interests together to discuss common issues or to map collaborative efforts. The Department of Education has brought together leaders of state educational technology efforts several times to share information and develop better collaboration. The National Science Foundation regularly convenes leaders of the research and policy communities to define important research agendas. In creating its national plan, the Office of Educational Technology has used electronic networks to convene practitioners to discuss issues of policy and practice. In Chapter Four, we suggested that a public-private organization be created to bring together the parties that must collaborate to produce effective educational software.

Leadership can also be provided by identifying and recognizing outstanding performance. One of the most powerful national programs affecting the private sector has been the Baldridge Awards for quality management. These awards have inspired many companies to undertake extensive efforts to improve the quality of performance of their entire organization. Various programs to recognize effective schools have had similar, if less well publicized, effects. Effectively publicized programs that appropriately recognize technology-enabled schools, effective educational software, or specific classes of educational technology applications can provide strong guidance and incentives to schools, school systems, and the private sector.

Creating and Disseminating Better Information for Reformers Concerning Technology. A traditional federal government function has been to survey activities across districts and states to understand what is working and what pitfalls and barriers exist. In the area of educational technology, the Department of Education might gather data and assess and disseminate information on

- effective strategies for financing educational technology at the state and district levels

- exemplary examples of program and schoolwide implementations of technology

- effective applications of technology to the training and professional development of teachers

- the progress in connecting schools and classrooms to the national information infrastructure

- the access of various special populations of students to technology.

Some of these are tasks for the National Center for Education Statistics; others would best be carried out by the Office of Education Research and Improvement (OERI) or the Planning and Evaluation Service. Many of the examples of effective practice would presumably be found in the pioneer schools and districts that are emerging.

Fostering the Development of More Effective Assistance Organizations. It is important to distinguish between the dissemination of information discussed in the previous subsection and the provision of assistance to schools, teachers, and school systems. RAND's experience in evaluating NASDC's program persuades us that there is an important function of organized assistance for the transformation of schools generally and for the development of schools with technology-enabled learning environments in particular. This assistance should be concrete, timely, and sustained. It should be provided on terms that the recipients find helpful, rather than on terms convenient to the provider.

NASDC is creating "design-based" assistance organizations. However, this is but one class of assistance organization. The Department of Education's Regional Laboratories are another, as are the myriad of assistance centers that support departmental programs. The nation's schools of education are potentially another source of such assistance.

The Department of Education should identify the qualities of effective assistance and inventory the potential sources of assistance related to technology. Working in conjunction with department offices, particularly OERI, it should guide the department's support of assistance organizations so as to further the effective school use of educational technology.

The medium is part of the message. The Department of Education should actively seek opportunities to model and exploit the use of technology as a tool in providing assistance.

Support for Research, Development, and Demonstration (RD&D). RD&D support has historically been one of the least controversial of federal roles. In areas where private firms cannot expect to capture the full benefit of their investment, R&D tends to be underfunded. Where states and localities have only limited RD&D management expertise, the federal government is the obvious source of support for R&D activities. This is true for education despite the fact that Congress has repeatedly resisted allocating significant funds to the Department of Education for the support of educational R&D.

Important educational technology capabilities can be traced to federal R&D efforts. DoD programs to develop technology-based training systems created much of the intellectual and organizational base for the development of CAI and the more recent integrated learning systems. The Internet is a product of NSF and DoD programs. The popular Mosaic browser for the World Wide Web was developed with federal funding. None of these products was directly targeted at K–12 education; all have or promise to have important impacts on that education.

Certainly there is little need for additional R&D on hardware or software products that have substantial application outside of education. The suppliers of such software and hardware products have every incentive to make R&D investments themselves. However, there are some needs specifically related to education, for which school demand does not seem currently adequate to justify private investment or for which the time horizons of public officials do not lead to state and local investment.

Reflecting our findings in Chapter Four concerning the market for content software, there may be a role for federal R&D supporting the development of software serving important educational needs, particularly in middle and secondary schools. Such developments should build on the substantial experience of the NSF in its mathematics and science education programs.

Chapter Four also argued that improved models for training teachers (and other staff) were needed as well as better methods for promoting their professional development after graduation. We are particularly attracted by the possibility that technology itself can provide more timely and relevant sources of information and assistance than is possible with current institutional arrangements. The report on teachers and technology by the Office of Technology Assessment identified a few examples of such R&D efforts. There should be more.

Earlier we suggested that the federal government investigate ways to promote equal access to educational technology by all citizens. Development and demonstration have important roles to play in this area.

Over the past two years, the Committee on Education and Training (CET) of the National Science and Technology Council has worked to coordinate the R&D agendas of the various departments that have interest in applying technology to education and training. This committee has established priorities for future work on learning and cognitive science R&D, new assessment methods, the development of software tools, and demonstrations of uniquely effective technology-enabled learning processes.[2]   Continued dialogue about R&D needs and opportunities is desirable.

We see special value in demonstrations that point the way to better uses of technology in education (and training). Such demonstrations can produce high-quality information concerning the potential of technology for the improvement of learning. Demonstration projects also provide a means for the federal government to share some of the risks associated with new ventures. Solicitations associated with such programs provide the opportunity to stimulate the development of effective new technology applications. Support for demonstrations, if properly structured, can also help with the development of new sources of assistance to schools and to teachers. The Technology Challenge Grant program authorized by Title III of the Improve America Schools Act is a good example of a demonstration program that should contribute to several of these goals.

We close by reiterating a theme we have tried to sustain throughout this report. The nation's most important educational goal must be to produce learners adequately prepared for life and work in the 21st century. Faced by uncertain demands, we should ensure that our youth master basic language and mathematics skills (perhaps in the context of studying subjects like history and science), but that they also learn how to gather information and collaborate with others in the use of that information in solving problems and making informed judgments on public and private concerns. The nation must develop schools that can enable our youth to meet these goals. Properly employed, educational technology will make a major contribution to those schools and their students.

---

[2]Committee on Education and Training, 1995, pp. 8–9.

PARTICIPANTS IN CTI WORKSHOPS

WORKSHOP ON IMPROVING SUPPLY OF EDUCATION SOFTWARE, NOVEMBER 4–5, 1993

Susan Ambron
Paramount Technology Group
Palo Alto, CA

Gary Boycan
Office, Secretary of Defense
Personnel and Readiness
Washington, D.C.

J. Dexter Fletcher
Institute for Defense Analyses
Alexandria, VA

Lawrence T. Frase
Div. of Cognitive and
Instructional Science
Educational Testing Service
Princeton, NJ

Edward Heresniak
McGraw-Hill
New York, NY

Alan M. Lesgold
L R D C
Univ. of Pittsburgh
Pittsburgh, PA

Nelson E. Bolen
The Mitre Corporation
Bedford, MA

Ed Fitzsimmons
Office of Science &
Technology Policy
The White House
Washington, D.C.

Philip Dodds
IMA
Annapolis, MD

Henry Kelly
Office of Science & Technology
Policy
The White House
Washington, D.C.

Arthur Melmed
The Institute of Public Policy
George Mason Univ.
Fairfax, VA

David J. McArthur
RAND
Santa Monica, CA

Thomas K. Glennan, Jr.
RAND
Washington, D.C.

Wallace H. Wulfeck
NAVPERSRANDCEN
San Diego, CA

Dr. Jim Schnitz
Jostens Learning Corporation
San Diego, CA

Cris Popenoe
Putnam New Media
Reston, VA

WORKSHOP ON TECHNOLOGY AND TEACHER PROFESSIONAL DEVELOPMENT, NOVEMBER 21–22, 1994

Karen Billings
Microsoft Corporation
Bellevue, WA

Kathleen Fulton
Office of Technology
   Assessment
Washington, D.C.

Thomas Glennan
RAND
Washington, D.C.

Jinny Goldstein
PBS
Washington, D.C.

James Harvey
James Harvey & Assoc.
Washington, D.C. 20036

Nancy Hechinger
The Edison Project
New York City, NY

Jonathan Hoyt
Office of Educational
   Technology
U.S. Dept. of Education
Washington, D.C.

Ann Lieberman
Teachers College
New York, NY

Elan Melmed
RAND
Santa Monica, CA

Susan Mernit
Scholastic, Inc.
New York City, NY

Donna Muncey
Ethnographer
St. Mary's, MD

Susanna Purnell
RAND
Washington, D.C.

Linda Roberts, Director
Office of Educational Technology
U.S. Dept. of Education
Washington, D.C.

Lydia Wells Sledge
Kentucky Department of
   Education
Frankfurt, KY

Gwen Solomon
Office of Educational Technology
U.S. Dept. of Education
Washington, D.C.

Mark Steinberger
New York City Central School
   District 4
Brooklyn, NY

Barbara Yentzer
National Education Association
Washington, D.C.

WORKSHOP ON PLANNING AND FINANCING
EDUCATION TECHNOLOGY,
DECEMBER 8–9, 1994

Mike Radlick
New York Dept. of Education
Office of Instruction & Program
  Development
Albany, NY

Wayne Fisher
Technology Center
Nebraska Dept. of Education
Lincoln, NE

Scott Howard, Superintendent
Perry Public Schools
Perry, OH

Ron Gillespie, Assist. to Supt.
Central Kitsap School District
Silverdale, WA

Michael Eason
Florida Dept. of Education
Tallahassee, FL

John Richards
Bolt, Beranek & Newman, Inc.
Cambridge, MA

Don Gips
FCC
Washington, D.C.

Karen Kornbluh
FCC
Washington, D.C.

Richard Varn
Univ. of Northern Iowa
Cedar Falls, Iowa

Bob Gillespie
Robert Gillespie Associates
Bellevue, WA

Rick Weingarten
Computing Research
  Association
Washington, D.C.

Lee McKnight
MIT
Cambridge, MA

Garry L. McDaniels
Skills Bank Corp.
Baltimore, MD

Sue Collins
Apple Computer
Medford, OR

Al Zeisler
AT&T
Berkeley, NJ

Linda Roberts, Director
Office of Educational Technology
U.S. Dept. of Education
Washington, D.C.

Herb Jacobson
U.S. Department of Education
Washington, D.C.

Kirk Winters
U.S. Department of Education
Washington, D.C.

George Sotos
U.S. Department of Education
Washington, D.C.

Keith Stubbs
U.S. Department of Education
OERI/National Library of
   Education
Washington, D.C.

Alan McAdams
Johnson Graduate School of
   Management
Cornell University
Ithaca, NY

Jim Harvey
Harvey & Associates
Washington, D.C.

Alex Poliakoff
U.S. Department of Education
Washington, D.C.

Gwen Solomon
Office of Educational Technology
U.S. Dept. of Education
Washington, D.C.

Arthur Melmed
The Institute of Public Policy
George Mason Univ.
Fairfax, VA

Thomas K. Glennan, Jr.
RAND
Washington, D.C.

WORKSHOP ON MARKET FOR EDUCATION SOFTWARE, FEBRUARY 2–3, 1995

Garry McDaniels
Skillsbank
Baltimore, MD

Marilyn Rosenblum
Broderbund Software
Petaluma, CA

Thomas Haver
William K Bradford Publishing
Acton, MA

Bruce Nelson
Novell Education Sales
Orem, Utah

Alan Lesgold
LRDC
Univ. of Pittsburgh
Pittsburgh, PA

Dana Simmons
Find/SVP
Ithaca, NY

Linda Roberts, Director
Office of Educational
   Technology
U.S. Dept. of Education
Washington, D.C.

Tom Glennan
RAND
Washington, D.C.

Arthur Melmed
The Institute of Public Policy
George Mason Univ.
Fairfax, VA

Jim Schnitz
EduQuest
Atlanta, GA

William Spencer
Simon & Schuster
Needham Heights, MA

Roger Rogalin
Association of American
   Publishers
New York, NY

Randy Pennington
Chancery
Bellingham, WA

Bob Dixon
National Center to Improve the
   Tools of Educators
Olympia, WA

Tom Miller
Find/SVP
Ithaca, NY

Ed Fitzsimmons
Office of Science & Technology
   Policy
The White House
Washington, D.C.

Jim Harvey
Harvey & Associates
Washington, D.C.

Sue Purnell
RAND
Washington, D.C.

Herb Jacobson
U.S. Dept. of Education
Washington, D.C.

Gwen Solomon
Office of Educational
  Technology
U.S. Dept. of Education
Washington, D.C.

Ellen Schiller
U.S. Dept. of Education
Washington, D.C.

George Sotos
U.S. Dept. of Education
Washington, D.C.

Jerry Comcowish
U.S. Dept. of Education
Washington, D.C.

Jonathan Hoyt
Office of Educational Technology
U.S. Dept. of Education
Washington, D.C.

Norris Dickard
U.S. Dept. of Education
Washington, D.C.

Sue Kamp
Software Publishers Association
Washington, D.C.

COSTS AND EFFECTIVENESS OF EDUCATION TECHNOLOGY, JUNE 1–2, 1995

Linda Roberts, Director
Office of Educational
   Technology
U.S. Dept. of Education
Washington, D.C.

Steve Carr
Blackstock JrHS
Ventura, CA

Bob Fazio, Principal
Christopher Columbus Middle
   School
Union City, NJ

Bill Hadley
Langley High School
Pittsburgh, PA

Barbara Means
SRI International
Menlo Park, CA

Martin Huntley
BBN
Cambridge, MA

James A. Kulik
Center for Research on
   Learning and Teaching
University of Michigan
Ann Arbor, MI

David Dwyer
Apple Computer
Cupertino, CA

Ed Fitzsimmons
Office of Science & Technology
   Policy
The White House
Washington, D.C.

Fred Carrig
Board of Education
Union City School District
Union City, NJ

John Gibson, Principal
East Bakersfield High
Bakersfield, CA

Susan Wolf, Principal
Northbrook Middle School
Houston, TX

Beth Stroh
Taylorsville Elementary School
Taylorsville, Indiana

Douglas Merrill
RAND
Santa Monica, CA

Dexter Fletcher
Science and Technology Division
Institute for Defense Analyses
Alexandria, VA

James Harvey
James Harvey & Assoc.
Washington, D.C.

Tom Glennan
RAND
Washington, D.C.

Luis Osin
LRDC (visiting address)
Univ. of Pittsburgh
Pittsburgh, PA 15260
(Centre for Educational
    Technology (permanent
    address)
    Ramat Aviv, Israel)

Arthur Melmed
The Institute of Public Policy
George Mason Univ.
Fairfax, VA

Lawrence T. Frase
Div. of Cognitive and
    Instructional Science
Educational Testing Service
Princeton, NJ

Anderson, Robert H., Tora K. Bikson, Sally Ann Law, and Bridger M. Mitchell, Christopher R. Kedzie, Brent Keltner, Constantijn W. Panis, Joel Pliskin, and Padmanabhan Srinagesh, *Universal Access to E-Mail: Feasibility and Societal Implications*, MR-650-MF, RAND, Santa Monica, CA, 1995.

Apple Computer, Inc., *Changing the Conversation about Teaching, Learning, and Technology: A Report on 10 Years of ACOT Research*, Cupertino, CA: Apple Computer, Inc., 1995.

Becker, H. J., *Analysis of Trends of School Use of New Information Technology*, Prepared for the Office of Technology Assessment, University of California, Irvine, CA, March 1994.

Beryl Buck Institute for Education, *Exemplary Approaches to Training Teachers to Use Technology*, Vol. 1, prepared for the Office of Technology Assessment, Washington, D.C., 1994.

Committee on Education and Training, *Strategic/Implementation Plan, FY 1995–1999*, January 24, 1995, pp. 8–9.

Cuban, Larry, *Teachers and Machines: The Classroom Use of Technology Since 1920*, Teachers College, Columbia University, NY: Teachers College Press, 1986.

Fletcher, J. D., D. E. Hawley, and P. K. Piele, "Costs, Effects and Utility of Microcomputer Assisted Instruction in the Classroom," *American Educational Research Journal*, 27, 1990, pp. 783–806.

Gerstner, Jr., Louis V., Chairman and CEO-IBM Corporation, Remarks at the National Governors' Association Annual Meeting, Burlington, Vermont, July 30, 1995.

Harvey, James (ed.), *Planning and Financing Educational Technology*, DRU-1042-CTI, RAND, Santa Monica, CA, March 1995a.

Harvey, James (ed.), *The Market for Educational Software*, DRU-1041-CTI, RAND, Santa Monica, CA, May 1995b.

Harvey, James, and Susanna Purnell (eds.), *Technology and Teacher Professional Development*, DRU-1045-CTI, RAND, Santa Monica, CA, March 1995.

Hayes, Jeanne, and Dennis L. Bybee, "Greatest Need for Educational Technology," paper prepared to support congressional testimony in March 1995, Quality Education Data, Inc., undated.

Keltner, Brent, and Randy Ross, *The Cost of School-Based Educational Technology Programs*, MR-634-CTI/DoED, RAND, Santa Monica, CA, 1996.

Kulik, James A., "Meta-Analytic Studies of Findings on Computer-based Instruction," in E. L. Baker, and H. F. O'Neil, Jr. (eds.), *Technology Assessment in Education and Training*, Hillsdale, NJ: Lawrence, Erlbaum, 1994.

Means, Barbara, and Kerry Olson, *Technology's Role in Education: Reform, Findings from a National Study of Innovating Schools*, Menlo Park, CA: SRI, September 1995.

Melmed, Arthur (ed.), *The Costs and Effectiveness of Educational Technology: Proceedings of a Workshop*, DRU-1205-CTI, RAND, Santa Monica, CA, November 1995.

National Center for Education Statistics (NCES), *America's Teachers: Profile of a Profession*, U.S. Department of Education, Washington, D.C., May 1993.

National Center for Education Statistics (NCES), *Digest of Educational Statistics*, U.S. Department of Education, Washington, D.C., 1994a.

National Center for Education Statistics (NCES), *The Condition of Education 1994*, U.S. Department of Education, Washington, D.C., 1994b.

National Center for Education Statistics (NCES), *Advanced Telecommunications in U.S. Public Schools, K–12*, U.S. Department of Education, Washington, D.C., January 1995a, p. 3.

National Center for Education Statistics (NCES), *Digest of Educational Statistics*, U.S. Department of Education, Washington, D.C., 1995b.

National Center for Education Statistics (NCES), *Projections of Education Statistics to 2005*, U.S. Department of Education, Washington, D.C., January 1995c.

National Commission on Excellence in Education, *A Nation At Risk*, Washington, D.C.: National Commission on Excellence in Education, 1983.

Newman, Dennis, "Computer Networks: Opportunities or Obstacles?", in Barbara Means (ed.), *Technology and Educational Reform*, San Francisco, CA: Jossey-Bass Publishers, 1994, pp. 57-80.

New York Times, "Apple Holds School Market, Despite Decline," September 11, 1995.

Princeton Survey Research Associates, *National Education Associations Communications Survey: Report of Findings*, Princeton, NJ, June 2, 1993.

Quality Education Data, Inc. (QED), *Technology in Public Schools, QED's 13th Annual Census Study of Public School Technology Use*, Denver, CO, 1994.

Raizen, Senta A., *Reforming Education for Work: A Cognitive Science Perspective*, Berkeley, CA: National Center for Research in Vocational Education, 1989.

Resnick, Lauren, "The 1987 AERA Presidential Address: Learning in School and Out," *Educational Researcher*, 16 (9), 1987a, pp. 13–20.

Resnick, Lauren, *Education and Learning to Think*, Washington, D.C.: National Academy Press, 1987b.

Ringstaff, Cathy, Jean Marsh, and Keith Yocum, *ACOT Teacher Development Center Annual Report: Year Two*, ACOT, Cupertino, CA, January 1995.

Ross, Randy, unpublished RAND research on the cost of implementing new American schools.

Rothstein, Randy, and Karen Miles, *Where's the Money Gone? Changes in the Level and Composition of Education Spending*, Economic Policy Institute, Washington, D.C., 1995.

Secretary's Commission on Achieving Necessary Skills, *What Work Requires of Schools: A SCANS Report for America 2000*, Washington, D.C.: U.S. Department of Labor, June 1991.

Software Publishers Association, *Report on the Effectiveness of Technology in Schools, 1990–1994*, Washington, D.C.: Software Publishers Assn., 1995.

Software Publishers Association, *SPA K–12 Education Market Report*, Washington D.C., July 1994, p. 61.

Special Issue on Educational Technologies: Current Trends and Future Directions, *Machine-Mediated Learning*, Vol. 4 (2&3), 1994.

Tyack, David, and Larry Cuban, *Tinkering Toward Utopia*, Cambridge, MA: Harvard University Press, 1995.

U.S. Congress, Office of Technology Assessment (OTA), *Teachers and Technology: Making the Connection*, OTA-EHR-616, U.S. Government Printing Office, Washington, D.C., April 1995.